DO
LESS

BE
MORE

Also by Martina Sheehan and Susan Pearse:

Wired For Life

One Moment Please

Please visit: www.hayhouse.co.uk

SUSAN PEARSE AND
MARTINA SHEEHAN

DO
LESS

BE
MORE

How to Slow Down
and Make Space for What Really Matters

HAY HOUSE

Carlsbad, California • New York City • London
Sydney •Johannesburg • Vancouver • New Delhi

First published and distributed in the United Kingdom by:
Hay House UK Ltd, Astley House, 33 Notting Hill Gate, London W11 3JQ
Tel: +44 (0)20 3675 2450; Fax: +44 (0)20 3675 2451; www.hayhouse.co.uk

Published and distributed in the United States of America by:
Hay House Inc., PO Box 5100, Carlsbad, CA 92018-5100
Tel: (1) 760 431 7695 or (800) 654 5126
Fax: (1) 760 431 6948 or (800) 650 5115; www.hayhouse.com

Published and distributed in Australia by:
Hay House Australia Ltd, 18/36 Ralph St, Alexandria NSW 2015
Tel: (61) 2 9669 4299; Fax: (61) 2 9669 4144; www.hayhouse.com.au

Published and distributed in the Republic of South Africa by:
Hay House SA (Pty) Ltd, PO Box 990, Witkoppen 2068
info@hayhouse.co.za; www.hayhouse.co.za

Published and distributed in India by:
Hay House Publishers India, Muskaan Complex, Plot No.3, B-2,
Vasant Kunj, New Delhi 110 070
Tel: (91) 11 4176 1620; Fax: (91) 11 4176 1630; www.hayhouse.co.in

Distributed in Canada by:
Raincoast Books, 2440 Viking Way, Richmond, B.C. V6V 1N2
Tel: (1) 604 448 7100; Fax: (1) 604 270 7161; www.raincoast.com

Cover design: Leanne Siu Anastasi; Internal design: Rhett Nacson; Typesetting:
Bookhouse, Sydney; Editing: Margie Tubbs; Author photo: Tanya Love Portrait

A catalogue record for this book is available from the British Library.

ISBN: 978-1-78180-987-7

Printed and bound in Great Britain by TJ International Ltd, Padstow, Cornwall.

Contents

-+ -+

The Exercises

Introduction

-+ -+

*'The do more with less' revolution has undervalued the
precious moments of idle time. Whether it's a queue in the
post office, a lunch break at a training program, or waiting
for a friend to join you for coffee, a break in proceedings
is like a red rag to a bull. The device comes out to fill this
seemingly useless moment with seemingly useful activity. Idle
time somehow earned itself a bad name, a label for laziness
or sloth. But it also means 'at rest', and this is something
that attention needs more than you may realise . . .*

*A brain in a state of forced focus operates very differently
to a brain set free. It's the difference between listening
to one instrument or a whole orchestra. In a busy mind,
attention jumps randomly from instrument to instrument,
creating a cacophony of noise that holds little pleasure and
delivers little reward. It's only when the busyness subsides
that attention opens widely enough to allow the rest of the
orchestra to join in. It's the synchrony of many parts working
in harmony that creates the magic.*

Extract from *One Moment Please: It's Time to Pay Attention*,
by Martina Sheehan and Susan Pearse, 2014

W e live in a world where busy is better, me-time is just a distant memory, and the human attention span rivals that of a goldfish. We need to stop. Literally. It's time to bring back silence, stillness and solitude.

Once you learn to indulge in the magnificently difficult art of doing nothing, amazing things return to your life. You rediscover your potential for brilliant and surprising ideas, you realise your own inner voice offers great guidance and deserves to be heard, and you reconnect with the flow of life, which offers a free ride if you take a moment to get on board.

If you're the sort who says: 'I'll wait until I have nothing to do until I do nothing,' then this book is for you. There is no better time than now to reclaim your right to do nothing, and we'll show you many practical ways to do that, even in a busy life.

Are you ready to come on a journey with us to reclaim idle moments, and get more out of life by doing less? This is more than an aspiration. This is a practical skill that can be relearnt. We'll be your companions, we'll share our stories, and we'll show you the way. In fact we are going to show you 21 ways! So buckle up and get ready to slow down. We hope you enjoy exploring the wonderful possibilities that open up when you embrace the art of doing nothing.

Chapter 1
Why Doing Nothing Matters

-+ -+

Wouldn't it be wonderful if a productivity coach told you that, today, you will achieve more by doing less? What if an innovation expert told you that the best way to have a good idea is to sit back and do nothing? Would you believe it if your favourite guru proposed one simple rule you could adopt right now for living a great life: stop trying so hard!

In fact, all these pronouncements are true. You are not at your best when you pack every moment of the day with more to do, but when you are willing to engage in intentional and indulgent periods of downtime. Don't let anyone tell you it's lazy to linger over a coffee while watching the parade of people passing the cafe; that gazing out the window daydreaming is a waste of time; or even that hanging out your washing while a report sits unfinished on your laptop is procrastination. These might just be the most important moments in your day.

There is a deep pool of discerning insight, surprising creativity and profound wisdom residing inside each of us. But it will rest there untapped, unseen and unheard, unless you reclaim the right to be idle from time to time. It's only when you untether your mind from the constant push and pull of daily tasks that another layer of depth bubbles to the surface. That's why so many people experience 'aha' moments in random places like the shower, looking out the window of a train, walking in nature, and while on holidays. A total transformation takes place in your brain when you slow down, look up, let go and fall silent.

In this book, we'll reveal the science that explains why 'doing nothing' is a bona fide strategy for achieving what you really want. We'll share stories to remind you that your greatest moments of clarity emerge when you gear down. And we'll explore the many ways to reacquaint yourself with the glorious power of being idle without going crazy!

+ Moments of inspiration

J.K. Rowling, author of the famous Harry Potter novels, is often asked what the inspiration was for her work. *Explaining where the story came from is always very difficult, because I don't really know. The idea came to me very suddenly on a train journey from Manchester to London in 1990.* This mysterious experience fascinates us because we've all had glimpses of it, even if it's not the prelude to a big life-changing shift. In an unexpected and seemingly inexplicable moment, things suddenly make sense, and all we can say is, 'I can't really explain it. It was like an epiphany. It just hit me!'

Maybe you were out for some exercise, or in the shower, or sitting in traffic then bam! An idea arrives as if from nowhere. It feels like a lightning bolt has struck and left behind a precious residue, a new perspective you couldn't see before that seemingly aimless moment. It might be a personal realisation that suddenly crystallises and can no longer be ignored: this is not the relationship for me! Or it could be a spark of inspiration about your work that now catapults you back into it with renewed energy and a clearer direction.

Whether these gifts from the ether are big or small, they always feel like important navigation points. They are different to solutions that emerge from a logical flow of thinking things through, or results that appear at the end of an intense period of effort. When you plan your holidays, respond to an email, or even just reflect on a meeting while sitting on the bus home, you can track the steps your thoughts take from start to finish. But when a leap of insight strikes, it's as mysterious as passing through a black hole. One moment you are just sitting quietly, and the next moment the world is irrevocably changed.

–+ –+

Isaac sat in his garden, as he did most afternoons, enjoying the changing colours of the sky. Birds flew past as they foraged for their last meal of the day, and the wind tickled the leaves of a laden apple tree. As he sat peacefully, his body was relaxed, his heartbeat was slow and steady, and his attention wandered gently across the vista below, captured by nothing in particular. In that moment, an apple fell from the tree. In Isaac's open and receptive state, the movement of the apple was recorded as more than just a trivial act of nature. Somewhere deep in the recesses of his brain a cascade of ideas, theories and notions that had been brewing for many years, but had remained jumbled like an unfinished jigsaw puzzle, suddenly found their missing piece: the theory of gravity.

–+ –+

If, rather than relaxing and doing nothing in particular, Sir Isaac Newton had been sitting in his garden dwelling on problems, running through his to-do list for the next day, or reviewing his unfinished papers trying desperately to unravel his long-sought solution, the falling apple would not have made its mark. At best he may have thought to himself: *It's time to harvest those apples*. Or he might have mindlessly picked it up and eaten it, or he may not have seen it at all. He probably would have walked away from his garden that afternoon, shoulders heavy, head hung low, and continued the hard slog of 'trying' to find the answer. In fact, if Newton was that sort of guy, he never would have visited his garden!

Many significant discoveries and momentous shifts in history involve similar stories. Sir Charles Darwin, famous for his theory of evolution, was known to work in his office for no more than four hours a day, spending the rest of his time walking in nature, writing letters, reading with his wife and resting. Both Newton and Darwin, like many other significant figures in history, were known for their strong work ethic and deep commitment to their search for understanding, so we could never accuse them of being lazy. Lucky for them, in their era resting, reflecting, and exploring things seemingly unconnected to their immediate work were considered important, even essential, activities that contributed to their goal—certainly not a waste of time.

What a shame that those who shape the modern work environment judge downtime to be 'dead time'; as if nothing of value occurs when you disconnect from plans, tasks, deadlines and expectations. While there's nothing wrong with hard work, dedication and effort, it's a mistake to believe they are the only ingredients required to 'produce the goods'. The greatest leaps forward, not just throughout history but for every one of us in our regular lives, rely on our willingness to stop and hear the whisper-quiet voice of our own deep knowledge and wisdom. Unless you value liberal doses of doing nothing, you're not giving your full potential the chance to emerge.

+ The answer lies in space

Having more, doing more, working more, worrying more, and trying more don't automatically lead to achieving more, experiencing more or enjoying more. In fact, the hustle and bustle of ceaseless activity and urgent expectation only serves to lift levels of stress, frustration, disappointment and unhappiness. Busyness is a barrier to self-reflection, a hindrance to novel solutions, and a smokescreen to clarity.

We all want to do more of the things that matter, and less of the things that don't. But doing more and more and more, just because it's there to be done, is not just a recipe for stress and exhaustion, it's also a pathway to mediocrity. In a state of busyness, you cannot access your best ideas, or distinguish between meaningful and meaningless tasks, or notice the subtle voice of intuition rising from the deep. In a state of busyness, your brain moves fast, skimming the tops of the waves, and grabbing a bite of everything in its path in a futile attempt to consume it all. At this speed your brain cannot digest what it takes in—let alone convert it into productive outcomes or useful ideas.

When you're in a state of constant action, you'll not only make mistakes and miss vital information, you'll lose all sense of discernment and do a lot of stuff that ends up being a waste of your precious energy. Tasks are ticked off not because they matter, but because ticking them off feels like progress. Choices are made, not because they are the ones that take you closer to your dreams, but because they are the easiest ones to make in that instant. There's no space to notice the golden opportunities, the magical moments, and the significant turning points that lie in wait to transform your day and your life.

This is the trap of living a busy life: there's no space. The moment a gap opens in the day, a busy person will fill it. And if it's not a physical task, it's a mental one. Idle moments are seen as wasted moments, but nothing could be further from the truth.

+ It's a lightning storm or it's fireworks

Your brain is never quiet. Electrical activity crackles constantly between neurons, whether you're awake, asleep, planning, listening, daydreaming or worrying. Lucky for us, we now live in a world where scientists have been able to map the different patterns of our brain activity against the various things we do in our lives. And one of the most fascinating discoveries is the pattern of activity that reveals itself when you do nothing in particular.

While you might think more goes on in there when you are busy, in fact the opposite is true. When you're engaged in goal-directed tasks or attention-demanding thoughts, very specific regions of your brain light up. This synchronised lightning storm is known as the Task Positive Network, and it reflects the concentration of energy flowing through regions of your brain associated with conscious mental processes like listening, planning, analysing, problem-solving and decision-making.

But when you sit back, look up and relax, that network quietens down and a different one comes to life. This is the Task Negative Network and, compared to the normal lightning storm that accompanies your day-to-day tasks, this network is more like New Year's Eve fireworks! With your attention no longer directed to something in particular, the electrical activity in your brain is free to flicker and flow broadly and deeply, activating regions often kept silent when you are busy, and connecting neurons that don't get a chance to share their information when you've got something else to do. No wonder the ideas and insights you have in Task Negative mode can be unexpected, novel and uniquely personal.

Activation of the Task Negative Network is associated with spontaneous recollections, improvisation and imagination, creative leaps, daydreaming, self-awareness and soul-searching, moral and emotional sensitivity, and the perceptive feelings we often label as intuition, insight or foresight. These rich rewards lie buried and out of reach when your Task Positive Network is in play. With all your neural energy absorbed by that lightning storm, the fireworks show is cancelled. Your Task Positive and Task Negative networks cannot both be active at the same time.

So that's why solutions to lingering problems drop into your mind when you're taking a shower. It's why those life-changing realisations happen during holidays. It's why indecision about which of the many tasks on your to-do list you should do first only resolves itself when you walk away from your desk. And it's why looking out the window of the train allows your imagination to deliver a fully-formed idea for a story.

It would be nice to think you could flip the switch between these two modes with ease. They're both important and one is not better than the other. They each have their place in a full and well-rounded mental life. But your Task Negative Network is particularly sensitive. It takes just the slightest distraction for it to go as quiet as a mouse, close up shop, and let the Task Positive Network steal the show.

Just consider the last time you were daydreaming. You might have been relaxing around the pool while on holiday, or maybe you were just looking out the window at work. Lost in another world, it only takes a loud bang or the call of your name and you are suddenly pulled from your reverie. In an instant, your Task Negative Network falls silent and, as you sit up, turn around and check what's happening, all your brain activity now flows through regions associated with your Task Positive Network. You are looking, listening, thinking, moving and responding to something in particular. Your attention is now busy with these tasks and has closed the door to reflections and musings for a while. It will feel like the ideas and dreams that had been dancing like butterflies before your eyes just a moment before have disappeared, frightened by the rustling of your mind, and are now nowhere to be found. If you try to recreate that same experience later, it can seem elusive. Even if you can settle back into the relaxed state required to switch off your Task Positive Network to allow your Task Negative Network to once again weave its magic, it will often take you wandering in new fields of ideas and imaginings.

Your Task Negative Network reflects activity in diverse parts of the brain, meaning that connections are often made between usually unrelated concepts. Rather than following a series of logical steps between a problem and a solution, long spindle cells bypass that lock-step process and present you with ideas that can sometimes seem impossible to explain. In fact, the best ideas and most novel solutions are often just elegantly simple combinations of factors that had not previously been noticed before. A true discoverer is one who fertilises their brain with many sources of diverse facts and concepts, then allows their clear mind and fresh eyes to weave them into a magical new vision.

We'll never know what aspect of the falling apple unearthed Newton's final piece of the gravity puzzle. We'll never know whether it was the rocking of the train or a glimpse of a particular building that shook Harry Potter into J.K. Rowling's consciousness. But we do know that it's essential to get out of the way if you want the deepest parts of your brain to join the party.

+ I did nothing, and nothing happened!

It's not actually the act of doing nothing that produces results. Doing nothing is just a doorway from one mental state to another, and it is the only way to reach the point where your Task Positive Network will release its control and allow your brain to start the fireworks show.

Scientists discovered the Task Negative Network, or what they generally call the Default Network, while studying brain activity in participants undertaking particular tasks. While the participants were resting between tasks, researchers kept recording their brain activity, and were surprised with what they found. Contrary to common belief and to what we might logically assume, when we do nothing we experience heightened levels of mental activity and predictable patterns in more regions of the brain than when we are involved in tasks.

But this shift in state is not immediate, and it is not guaranteed. Even just subtle intentional actions or thoughts can keep you in Task Positive mode. Just because you appear to be physically doing nothing, you may be mentally doing a whole lot. Sitting on the bus and looking out the window could mean you are re-running a situation from earlier in the day that caused you frustration. You may be mulling over why someone made a decision and how you wish you had responded. These circling thoughts capture your attention, and it is your Task Positive Network that remains highly engaged during this process. The same is true if you are waiting at a cafe for a friend to arrive and scrolling through your newsfeed or playing a game on your device. By looking, tapping and responding, you continue to use the same parts of the brain used in normal daily tasks, so you are not idling. You are also keeping your Task Positive Network switched on if you stare at the work in front of you and try really hard to come up with a good idea.

Any feeling that you are directing your attention and 'thinking it through' is a sign that you are working with logical and methodical mental processes, not cracking open the door for leaps of insight and novel ideas. Busy people, and people with busy minds, rarely experience the peaceful sensation that arises when the Task Positive Network releases its grip. Just as the lull that precedes the first spark of the Task Negative Network settles over them, a task, a thought or a distraction jumps in to steal the moment.

When you truly settle into the act of doing nothing, a cascading series of physiological changes takes place in your body and brain. Each step in this transformation is essential, if you are to reach the moment when an inspiration, and insight, or idea actually arises. The first step is to detach your attention from whatever you are doing. Mostly this will mean sitting back, lifting your head or walking away from a task, but it can also just mean flicking your eyes up, taking a deep breath, and pausing for a moment with your attention gently resting in the present. If you are able to pause patiently in this idle moment and keep your attention from immediately reattaching itself to something else, you have a chance of continuing the steps.

Next in the cascade will be a slowing down and subtle relaxation of the body. This activates your parasympathetic nervous system, lowering your blood pressure and heart rate, and spreading a calm and peaceful glow through your body.

A relaxed body is a sign of a relaxed mind, which is essential for releasing the grip of your Task Positive Network. Once it goes silent, it is possible to move to the next step; there is now a clear space for your Task Negative Network to come to life and ignite connections deep within your brain. There waits a melting pot of profound wisdom, bubbling with ideas and insights. It is not known why only a few of these precious gems rise to conscious awareness, or what determines which ones see the light of day, but it is undoubtedly a fact that doing less is a precondition for many powerful revelations.

It can all happen in a split second if you have the patience, the faith and the fortitude to embrace idleness as a valid and valuable addition to a full life. But if the cascade of steps is interrupted at any point, you go straight back to square one. Once something in particular captures your attention, you will be pulled out of your reverie and left with only the solutions that can be found within your brain's Task Positive Network.

+ Finding the right path

This experience happens to us all, not just those famous few who have made a global mark on our thinking. Truths are realised when you are casually wandering, idly sitting, or curiously observing. Baffling though it may be, it seems that the fastest way to find direction when you're lost in a fog of confusion is to simply stop trying. In fact, you often create your own fog precisely **because** you're trying too hard!

-+ -+

Since she had turned sixty, this CEO had been talking about retiring. Her three-year contract as a chief executive was due to end within the year; her first grandchild had just been born; and her husband had been retired for over a year. It all sounded ideal. But she was concerned that her firm would struggle to find a candidate to fill her role in the timeframe required, and was talking about how she might just do just one more year to help them wrap up a few important projects she had on the go. She'd concocted a very intricate plan that she intended discussing with her Board in the coming months but, even by her own admission, it was driven by a sense of responsibility—and probably by a bit of fear of not having something to keep her busy. In the same breath as she outlined this plan, she also talked about her desire to travel for six weeks the following year, be a grandmother once a week, and that she was really, really tired. In her search for a logical way to tick every box, she had only served to whip up a mental dust storm. It was clear to everyone except her that there was something major missing in her plan. Clarity resurfaced when she was asked one simple question: 'Deep down, when you put everyone else's needs aside, what do you really, really want?' She paused . . . 'I really want to stop.'

–+ –+

Those critical turning points in life—whether it's time to change jobs, move house, get married, leave a relationship, take on a new business partner or retire—always seem to generate more questions than answers. You gather inform-ation, consider the pros and cons, garner other people's opinions, draw up plans, explore alternatives, but often delay the big decision in the hope that something will stand out among all the noise to point the way. While a certain amount of research, analysis and pondering is essential fodder to fertilise the rich field of ideas and insights that can be born in your quiet mind, in the end the proverbial arrow indicating which way you should go only emerges from the fog when you fall still and stop trying. Waiting there all along, like a steady compass needle, is a deep knowing of the answer and it emerges fully-formed: *I can't really explain it, but I know what I really want/what I am here for/what I need to do next.*

+ Small moments matter

Just allowing yourself to settle willingly into a short idle moment can be the most effective strategy to get through a busy day. 'I had to turn around and go back two times!' She was updating the group on her latest client event and explaining how, after it had finished, she had packed the car and headed towards home. Only a few blocks away from the venue, she suddenly had a thought: *Did I put the speakers in the car?!* In an instant she knew that she hadn't, so she turned back, snuck into the venue and picked up her speakers from near the doorway where she had left them. As she returned to the car and put them down to unlock it, one of the participants saw her and came over to say how much she had appreciated all her work. They had a lovely chat and she jumped back in her car, hitting the road home again. Yes, you guessed it! The speakers were still sitting where she had left them next to the car and, once more, her mind could only alert her to this fact when she reached that point in the drive where she had stopped rushing and let go of all the fast-moving busy thoughts that were blocking her from seeing what was right in front of her.

These important navigation points are essential, whether they are shining a light on a crucial life decision, or just helping you to see which task you need to focus on next. Even just lifting your head and scanning your environment, when you reach a point in your work where you feel unclear about which direction to go next, can be enough to help you locate your next point and kick off a fresh wave of activity. Standing up and walking away from a task, stretching your body and coming back to survey your handiwork, can reveal a spot that needs just a little more attention. Going for a walk at lunchtime can boost your energy and make the afternoon flow more easily. Looking out the window of the bus can help you arrive home with a clear mind. Sitting in your garden watching the changing colours of the late afternoon sky can produce a grand realisation about life. Escaping to the coast or the hills for a weekend can put your whole business into perspective and change your future.

'My head seemed a lot clearer when I returned from my holiday.' Our client had just finished talking about his wonderful trip, with amazing experiences like looking down from the rim of an active volcano and walking through forests alive with rare wild creatures. 'I walked into the office and I just sensed that we needed to shift our focus. As soon as I looked at the data on our markets, I could pinpoint the thing that was niggling me. So the plan I had before I left has been adjusted, and we are making some different decisions. I'm also making some changes in my own routines, to ensure I don't slip back into the day-to-day detail like I was before. Keeping a clear mind is undoubtedly the most important contribution I can make to this business.'

We all have a different structure to our days—different pressures, different occupations and very different person-alities. Creating your own pattern that balances 'doing something' and 'doing nothing' is important, because they are both vital for life. No-one can dictate what your perfect mix will be, but you can be sure that your life needs healthy doses of doing nothing. Maybe you would benefit from idle moments scattered through a busy day, or idle gaps when you can settle for longer into curious musings and wonderings; or maybe you crave intentional stretches of silence, stillness and solitude to indulge in self-reflection? For most of us, it's a combination of all these opportunities to rest and reach deep within that will serve us best.

The search for the sweet spot between activity and rest, moving and idling, focusing and daydreaming, and stress and relaxation can be challenging in a world where no-one wants to waste a minute. Living fully is a light dance through all these states, flowing from one to the other, tapping into the full depth of your potential and bringing it out into the world. But there are forces working against you, and understanding those forces is the first step toward reclaiming the best of yourself.

Chapter 2
Why Doing Nothing is Difficult

-+ -+

+ But what am I supposed to do?

The tension in the room was palpable. Colleagues were standing in pairs, some talking, some not. While those in conversation were smiling and animated, the silent pairs were clearly uncomfortable. It was a simple activity conducted for a leadership workshop, in which pairs shared their thoughts on a particular topic without any preparation time. As the first pair finished, they turned and one asked, 'What do we do now?'

'Just stand where you are and wait for the others to finish.' Well, you would have thought they'd been asked to stand in the centre of a speeding lane of traffic! They shuffled from one foot to the other, folded and unfolded their arms, lowered their heads, avoided eye contact with each other, and glanced regularly at the still talking pairs, no doubt hoping this would motivate them to finish more quickly. In turn, the pairs finished their conversations and joined the waiting game. And as the final pair fell silent, there was a collective sigh. It felt like someone had finally opened a valve and released the pressure. Their shoulders relaxed, they lifted their heads to look around, smiles touched their faces again, and as they looked to the front we asked, 'Who found it difficult to just wait with nothing to do?' Hands rose and heads nodded.

Amid the many challenges in our complex and fast-changing world, how can it be that the simple act of 'doing nothing' might have become one of the hardest things to do? Surely we all wish for moments in our day when we might be left alone without any expectation to do something, solve something, or respond to something? But faced with the bare and empty moment, rather than basking in the stillness, most people baulk.

In fact, researchers at Harvard University and the University of Virginia found that people will take some pretty extreme measures to fill this vacant space. Subjects were asked to spend just fifteen minutes alone with no distractions: no devices, no music, no paper or pen, no pictures on the wall, no items to touch and no windows to look out. A bare and empty room except for one button. Touching this button would deliver a light electric shock, which they had all previously experienced and reported as 'unpleasant'. Can you guess what happened? An extraordinary two-thirds of men and a quarter of women chose to give themselves electric shocks rather than sit without distraction. One high achiever shocked himself 190 times in just fifteen minutes![1]

+ Can you do nothing?

Have you tried to 'do nothing' lately? You may not have been tested by a completely empty room, but maybe you've stood for a few moments waiting for your takeaway coffee, or arrived early to a meeting and waited alone in the room, or suddenly found yourself in a quiet house after the family have headed off to their various activities. Or maybe you've sat on the sidelines at your child's weekend sport, or been stuck in a traffic jam. What did you do? Did you pick up your mobile device, turn on the TV or radio, ring someone, read some work materials, quickly dash through one or more things on your to-do list, or ponder your latest difficult problem?

The compulsion to fill every moment with activity is a dangerous trap. While cramming in one more task may feel useful, productive, even satisfying, it's not always the best use of an idle moment. In fact, cramming more in will inevitably lead you to a place where you become less productive, less creative, less inspired and less satisfied with life.

At a recent conference, a mumpreneur who had won the top award at the same event the year before was telling the group how she had started her business two years ago, after her second baby was born. Creating a line of gentle cleansing baby products, her business had taken off quickly, and she'd had great feedback. At a casual dinner later that night, she opened up a little more. 'I started with such enthusiasm and I've always been happy to do the long hours to keep up with demand. But lately I've found it tough. I feel like I'm on a treadmill, putting in so much energy, but standing still. I can't come up with the sort of creative ideas I used to have. Each night when I fall into bed, I have just a moment of wondering if there is a different way to achieve more. But by then I'm too tired to think about it.'

An increase in working hours not only lowers productivity, it can lead to negative productivity.[2] That sounds pretty extreme, but we all know that our cognitive resources have their limits. When you've been putting in long hours for days on end, or when you're under pressure and just can't get things off your mind, the clarity and focus you are able to bring to each task rapidly declines. That's when mistakes are made, vital information is missed, and the quality of your decisions deteriorates. Once you have to retrace your steps, fix up errors, or throw something out and start again, you're officially in negative productivity and you'll rightly feel like you're making no headway. In fact you're going backwards.

You would think this frustrating experience would be enough to make smart people stop, take stock, and find a better way to move through life. But this is the irony of the state of mind you enter when you're busy, overloaded and under pressure. It's difficult to see any option other than trying harder, getting up earlier, moving faster, taking short-cuts, and pushing through to the other side. The capabilities you rely on to make wiser choices are switched off. In fact, you become measurably dumber!!

Various studies reveal that multi-taskers experience a decline in IQ of up to fifteen points. Even facing the temptation to multi-task can reduce your IQ by ten points. So it's not surprising that busy people often make silly mistakes and bad choices.[3]

It's not only busy professionals who suffer from the blockages formed by doing too much. Sadly, it is now also becoming clear that the wondrous creativity of young children declines markedly once they start formal schooling. Overscheduled and overstimulated, the marvellous gifts of play, boredom, and imaginative wonderings necessary for them to develop their complete self are being overlooked in a world that places far too much value on activity.[4]

An exhausting compulsion to fill every moment with 'doing something' has spread like a rash through society. No matter what age, gender, work status, role or level of responsibility, people from all walks of life seem to have become really, really good at keeping busy. In fact 'doing nothing' doesn't even seem to be a viable option.

'Got a busy day?' the waitress asked, as I sat in the cafe. 'No,' I answered. She did a double take at this unexpected, and probably extremely uncommon, answer. 'That would be nice.' Always interested in how people react to this topic, I took it one step further. 'I purposely make it that way.' She gave a light laugh and an off-hand toss of her head: 'I could never do that. If I had any time to spare I'd be doing the housework!' Then she wandered back to the cafe's kitchen.

Why is it so difficult to face an empty moment between tasks in stillness and silence? Are we attracted to constant activity for some very good reason, or are we avoiding the void? It's likely to be a combination of both.

+ Avoiding the void

Some people genuinely fear what may arise if they are left with only their own thoughts for company. But research on mind wandering suggests that most people are happy daydreamers, indulging in 'positive constructive daydreaming.' They use their periods of freedom of thought to create vivid imagery of a desired future and imagine possibilities for moving towards it. In fact, children who develop and nurture this capability have a stronger statistical chance of future success.[5]

When you consider the physiological changes that take place as you move into a contemplative state, it makes sense that it is more likely to generate positive emotions. The body relaxes as a prelude to the connections generated in the mind, and this means that stress and anxiety are not dominating the scene. Sure, if you're out of practice, doing nothing will initially be uncomfortable. Your brain will use the empty space to search for the next problem to which it can apply itself, in the fast and busy way you've trained it to move.

If an idle moment just gives you more time to ruminate on worries, deadlines and to-do lists, that's a sure sign that your Task Positive Network is still in charge. During the electric shock study mentioned earlier, one round had to be abandoned when the researcher unintentionally left a pen in the room. He returned to find the study participant busily writing a to-do list!

It takes a very conscious choice and a bit of practice to let yourself settle into stillness before your Task Positive Network will get out of the way and allow the space for the Task Negative Network to weave its magic. But let's be honest, not every realisation that arises when you slow your mind down will be welcome. Deep self-reflection, listening to the voice within, and a willingness to face the truth will sometimes unearth a message you thought you didn't want to hear. It may be a recognition that it's time to make a tough change in your life; or an idea that means you'll have to throw away years of hard work; or an insight that it's time to let go of something that may feel safe, but could be holding you back. The irony is that ignoring the truth within does not make it go away. These are signposts that suggest the possibility of something more meaningful, authentic and fulfilling, and they tend to keep returning until you act on them. While acknowledging them and acting on them may seem painful, ignoring them will just unleash a game of cat and mouse, as you seek to evade your own voice and its inescapable message.

In her early twenties, she moved with her then-boyfriend to live in a new city. They set up home, both found good jobs, and were enjoying their new lifestyle very much. About one year later, out of the blue, he proposed to her.

I remember the moment as clearly as if it were yesterday. It's not so much what he said or did that I remember, it's how I responded. As the word 'yes' came out of my mouth, a second voice deep inside me said, 'But I'm never going to marry him.' At the time I ignored it and, for more than a year, I embraced life as a happy fiancée, or so it would have seemed from the outside. I felt like a phoney every time someone admired my lovely engagement ring; I deftly avoided questions about wedding plans and I buried myself in my career. Not even my closest friends or family would have thought that there was anything amiss and, more importantly, I didn't even acknowledge it myself. I avoided any reflections on the future because every time I went there, that inner voice was telling me that this was not the path for me.

So she kept herself busy, defiantly avoiding the void, and played along with each of the steps that presented themselves until, inevitably, the fork in the road left her with no choice. Her fiancé was offered a job in another city and they were moving. They visited the new city, found an apartment, moved their furniture in and he started his job. But she kept her job in their former city and commuted on weekends. 'I'm doing so well here, I don't want to leave just yet, but I will look for another job soon,' she would say. The crunch came one day at the airport, as she was dropping him off after a weekend together. 'I'm not coming,' she said. It was a cruel way to break the news, and a terrible process to then disentangle their lives. *If I had listened earlier to my own inner voice, I could have avoided not only the pain caused to another by my inaction, but also the difficulties I experienced over the coming months and years trying to find a path that felt truly right for me.*

+ Attraction to action

While some people may intentionally be avoiding the void, for many of us it's more about being a bit too attracted to action. If you find it more comfortable to fill an idle moment with something else to do, you're likely to have acquired a strong habit of diving from one thing to the next with little pause, believing this is what makes things happen.

When we asked the leaders in the workshop what they experienced while standing quietly (in their case for no longer than four minutes) they shared the following comments:

- *I felt so uncomfortable, like I was doing something wrong and that someone would see me just standing there and wonder why I wasn't doing something.*
- *It was like standing on stage and I felt really exposed, like everyone was looking at me.*
- *I just started thinking of all the things I'll have to do when I get back to my desk. There will be so many emails and I'll be up late tonight dealing with them. That made me feel stressed, and then I got really annoyed at you!*
- *I'm so shocked at how I felt. It really hit me that I never, ever truly do nothing. It was the strangest feeling and it's a bit scary. I never thought I was addicted to being busy, but now I know I am.*

Anything habitual and familiar becomes easier, whether it's good for you or not. A busy person tends to get busier. Whether it's the grip of habit, the pleasure of fleeting reward, the fear of missing something, the comfort of routine, or the badge of honour, busyness has been mistaken for progress and achievement.

+ Keeping things moving

'Do you have to do that right now?' There was a touch of frustration in her voice as she challenged him. They'd just come back to the house after dropping some clothes at a charity store, and they'd planned to make a nice healthy lunch and take a break before the next round of activity. They were moving out of their house and the list of things to do was long, and getting longer. But he'd bowled into the house and headed straight to the stereo system, which was now lying in pieces on the floor. 'I just need to keep things moving,' he explained.

'Keeping things moving' feels like making progress. Finishing a task and ticking it off the list feels good. Even moving a project from one stage to the next is deliciously rewarding. But how often does all your energy and effort really make a dent in the things that matter most? Are you falling for the false high of busyness and missing the slow burning glow of true fulfilment?

Your brain has a lot to answer for in this deceit. In direct response to our evolutionary success, the reward response in the brain is much more responsive to fast-moving results than slow, deep contentment.

Completing a task, however trivial, literally gives you a high. Whether it's scratching something off your to-do list; cleaning out your email inbox; scoring points in an online game; or checking your social media posts and finding a few likes and comments—each of these situations triggers a chemical shift in your brain. Your reward system is highly reactive to simple actions that get a quick result, no matter how meaningful. A delicious dollop of feel-good chemicals floods your brain, and it is the desire to repeat this reward that drives you to seek more of these 'achievement' moments. This means you will experience a real sense of satisfaction when you complete something, whether it's reading an email from a customer saying how your business has changed their life, or the moment you finish putting all the dirty dishes in the dishwasher.

Your brain doesn't make any distinction between a goal that was meaningful and the completion of a mundane task on your to-do list. You need to make those distinctions yourself and, when you're busy, you're less likely to sort the wheat from the chaff. Impulse control is one the first things you lose when you're overloaded. So rather than asking the question about where you'll achieve the greatest return for your time and attention, you're more likely to just grab the next quick task and get it done. Challenges that deserve deeper reflection and slower consideration are often put off, because they appear not to offer an immediate return. But they might be the ones with greater potential impact in the long term.

Just to be sure you stay on track, your brain has another clever trick: if you leave tasks undone, it makes you feel uncomfortable. Uncertainty, feeling out of control, or having something left unfinished are just a few of the things that trigger the brain's threat response. Rather than feeling the contentment of reward chemicals, you are flooded with cortisol and its companion stress hormones, and they trigger feelings of alertness and anxiety. This is your brain's way of making you deal with something and, until you do, the feelings will persist. Your Task Negative Network cannot compete in this environment and will stay stubbornly quiet to allow you to address the perceived danger. Of course the danger is rarely real, but it takes a clear presence of mind to recognise this and go against the brain's loud call to action. Only those with well-honed impulse control can comfortably leave something unfinished until later and sit back, rest and reflect instead.

Keeping busy and active has become a comfortable habit for so many of us. It does not take long to train your brain to adopt a habit, then when you throw in the chemical mix from the threat and reward systems, the habit of busyness is an easy one to learn. Going 'off habit' feels uncomfortable. Your brain urges a return to the known, and rewards you by making things feel normal again. "But I get so bored when there's nothing to do. I can't stand it!" She was completing her post-graduate studies part time while working in a demanding role, and she genuinely felt that she was good at doing lots of things at once. But now she understood that this feeling of boredom was also a trap, constantly coercing her to take on more. She was losing the ability to enjoy her downtime, even finding the trip home on the bus felt like a slow and frustrating waste of time, to be endured only with her trusty device at hand.

If you run too fast from feelings like boredom and discomfort, you run straight back into the arms of mindless habits, and you become less and less likely to experience your own version of life's falling apple. Indulging in the productive and empowering act of doing nothing is a matter of choosing a new habit that, over time, will become a valued tool in your armoury of productivity, fulfilment and achievement.

There are so many forces pushing us all to do more, keep moving, catch up, go faster and never stop. But they are all misleading myths, brain traps and bad habits. You **can** do nothing and achieve more, and you can do it without going crazy!

Chapter 3
How to Do Nothing

-+ -+

*I*f you've made it this far, it's probably fair to say you believe a bit more downtime would be a valuable addition to your life. But maybe you have some concerns, doubts or even disbelief that it is possible for you to really fit it in. When you take a good look at all the things you're doing, there's probably not much that initially seems like a complete waste of time, otherwise you would already have stopped doing it. I bet you can find a seemingly valid reason for everything on your to-do list, and a reasonable justification for why you squeeze just a bit more in whenever you have an idle moment.

Let's face it, there will always be many more things to do in a day than you can ever expect to achieve. With all the best intentions in the world, no-one could possibly address everything that clamours for their attention. Working faster, longer and harder to do it all might be your first inclination. But this is heading in the wrong direction. The question should not be: *How can I find a way to squeeze more in?* Try instead: *How can I be sure I'm doing the things that matter most?*

The truth is that a very small percentage of the things that you think you should do will make any real difference in the long run. The Pareto Principle suggests that about 80% of your results come from 20% of your efforts. But when your brain gets hell-bent on chewing through tasks, it seems easier to just do everything than to take stock and try to figure out which of the 20% is worthwhile.

Unfortunately, there isn't a simple way to work it out. Your rational brain will come up with a reason to do just about anything that is presented. In fact it is, more often than not, the real culprit in the theft of your precious opportunities to be idle. Hidden beneath all the planning, analysing and rationalising, the deeply instinctive gut offers quiet guidance. It's the voice you remember later, after you've had to redo some work, or after someone changes a plan that you'd already put heaps of effort into, or after you've had to turn back to retrieve a forgotten item. 'I **knew** that was going to happen!' you moan.

There are simple and practical ways to reconnect with this part of yourself, and to find the life where meaning, inspiration and fulfilment lie in full sight, rather than beneath a shroud of busyness. Let's find out how.

+ Building a habit of doing nothing
Do you believe that fresh ideas, deep insights, intuition and wise realisations have value? Do you believe that they can fast track you to a place of achievement and sidestep the

long hours of effort? Do you believe that some of your best contributions and untapped potential rest hidden deep inside, and that accessing them will enhance your life? The science is clear and it offers a new understanding and appreciation of the fact that something rich and precious is on offer when you do nothing.

This knowledge can motivate you to move forward and embrace a life where you aim to do less, but the next step requires a bit more resolve. It's all about changing habits, an uncomfortable and initially unrewarding experience! This is where the real work takes place, and where simple disciplines, the willingness to sit with discomfort, and the faith to act without expectation are essential. Every exercise we offer in this book is designed specifically to help guide you through the challenges presented when you start changing habits.

Be warned; your brain will resist. Remember it already has a tendency to be easily captured by the lure of action, but it also has a natural resistance to changing habits. Your neural pathways are already knitted together in networks that reflect your current ways of doing things and, the stronger the habit, the more dominant the neural pathway. Going 'off habit' requires extra mental effort, and this is something your brain is physiologically designed to resist. Doing something new therefore feels uncomfortable and wrong.

This is why you'll need to remind yourself regularly why it's worth persevering. Why is it important? What possibilities might emerge if you can build this new habit? How will your life be different, and what are the benefits? Think about these questions and find a compelling motivation that you can reflect on regularly. It could be about spending more quality time with loved ones, finally achieving a long-held dream, finding space to work out what you really want to achieve, engaging more actively in parenting at a crucial time in your children's lives, getting fit and healthy, or just feeling more at peace with your life. Whatever it is for you, write it down, stick it on your fridge or make it a screensaver on all your screens. We all work best when guided by a higher purpose than just getting through the day. Keep your eye on the bigger picture and you'll find it much easier to keep going.

Until a new behaviour is repeated enough times to grow a new neural pathway in your brain, it will continue to feel odd. And that's why so many efforts to change habits ultimately fail. But discomfort is not a sign that something is wrong or that you are no good at it. It's a sign that you are growing, changing and making a real difference to your life. Repetition is the key to building new pathways in the brain and, once they have been trodden again and again, a new behaviour starts to feel normal and comfortable. Quite often this happens suddenly. One day you'll realise that it feels quite okay to pause, sit idly and allow your ideas to bubble up, without having to jump straight into the next task!

One of the best pieces of advice we can offer on changing habits is this: focus only on the habit you want to create, not the habit you want to stop. Positive focus is always more powerful than negative. So never, never, never berate yourself for slipping back into old habits, **because it will happen**. Simply notice if it does, then bring the new habit to mind and look for the next opportunity to try again.

And finally, enjoy the journey. Celebrate. Be proud of any step you take, no matter how small. Your brain changes every day and no effort is wasted. Create the life you want by choosing to live it now.

The Exercises

-+ -+ -+ -+ -+ -+ -+ -+ -+ -+ -+ -+ -+ -+ -+ -+

Slowing down, saying no, sitting still . . . and many other ways to do less and be more

21 Ways to Do Less and Be More

-+ -+

*I*t's important to remember that doing nothing is not about seeking or digging for the ideas, insights and inspiration you want to have. It's about creating the conditions that allow the door to these rich rewards to swing open. Once the door opens, you cannot predict what you will see on the other side. Attend simply to the goal of getting better at opening the door. Each of the exercises you'll find here plays a part in helping you develop greater ease with the various complex challenges you might face in just letting that door open.

We all face our own unique combination of challenges, and you'll find some of these exercises easy and some of them more difficult. We offer them because we've learnt (quite often the hard way!) that you can't just wait and hope for the perfect conditions to arise in a busy life. You need to be intentional about how you create your day, how you make your choices, and how you respond to situations. You'll have heard of many of these exercises or a variation of them, and you've probably tried a few of them before. Regardless, try them all, even if you think there are some you don't need. They are all designed to refine skills that help you access your best potential and achieve more.

Many of the exercises focus purely on slowing down. This in itself takes presence of mind and a good dose of impulse control. When all about you are moving fast, demanding action and spreading a virus of urgency, it is usually the one who can pause amid it all who'll see a pathway, choose wisely and provide leadership. Other exercises help you to develop comfort with situations that are becoming increasingly foreign, particularly silence, solitude and space. They are sorely-needed retreats that you can find within your normal daily life, rather than waiting until a holiday or planned break, and they are all vital conditions for a flourishing brain.

We'll also guide you through the difficult tasks of saying 'no', letting things go, and working out what **not** to do. And if it all sounds like hard work, it's not. In fact we invite you to walk away and play much more often than you probably do now, because it's a proven pathway to enhance your creativity **and** expand your happiness.

Each exercise starts with a mantra of sorts. When you change the way you think about a situation or a challenge, you will find it so much easier to change your actions. In fact, changing the way you think will automatically open up a whole range of new options you may not have noticed before. So use these mantras to break old patterns of thinking that could be holding you back, and to create new ones that will help you design the life you really want.

Activity does not always equal achievement, but it should. Don't pour your heart and soul into things that make little difference. Your precious attention, your vital energy and your limited time are tools for bringing the best of yourself to the world. It takes just a moment to see the truth, to find direction, and to dream big. The only thing that is asked of you is to stop and listen. So indulge in the magnificent art of doing nothing whenever you can.

-+ -+

Wherever you are, be all there!

-+ -+

Jim Elliot,
Christian missionary

Exercise 1
Pay Full Price

-+ -+

Doing one thing well is better than doing many things poorly.

Are you a crazy, busy, champion multi-tasker? They're the ones who have something bubbling on the stove while talking on the phone, replying to an email, and mouthing instructions at family members. They've got more to get done than there are hours in the day, and believe the only way to get through it all is go fast and hard. In some strange way they feel quite comfortable with it. In fact they think they're pretty good at it, and maybe deep down they believe they thrive in it.

'I could not get my kids out the door in the morning if I didn't do a million things at once,' young mum exclaimed, throwing her hands in the air. 'I get them breakfast while packing their lunch boxes, sipping coffee and taking bites of toast (which I never finish), with one ear listening to the news and my mind planning what to wear to work today.' Despite being exhausted before she even left the house, she was proud of what she could achieve. She wears her Supermum status like a badge of honour.

I suppose it's a logical question in this busy world: *Why do one thing when you can do five?* There is no doubt that certain activities can be undertaken in parallel, but only those that don't cause conflict within the brain. For example, you can walk and chat with someone at the same time. You can read and drink coffee at the same time. But the truth is that, even in these simple cases of multi-tasking, your brain is switching between them, and little pieces of awareness are lost. These attention gaps become more pronounced as you attempt to juggle more and more. Soon you will miss vital information, make mistakes you won't find until later, and offend someone without even realising it.

Many people embrace multi-tasking with pride, but is it the timesaving, productivity-boosting tool it promised to be? The short answer is 'no'. For more than a decade now, research has shown that multi-tasking is far less productive than doing one thing at a time. In fact, it can take you 1.5 times longer to do your tasks when you are multi-tasking.[1] There is no greater strategy for productivity than doing one thing at a time—mindfully and with full awareness.

'Not for me,' I hear you say. 'I'm great at it. I've had loads of practice and I get so much done.' It might feel like that but, once again, your brain has sucked you into believing the myth that 'keeping things moving = progress'.

In one particular study, groups were compared based on their tendency to multi-task and their belief that it boosted their performance. The self-proclaimed expert multi-taskers were found to be **worse** at multi-tasking than those who did a single thing at a time![2]

Brains are not the super computers we might wish them to be; they aren't designed to be juggling many things at once. Multi-tasking causes mental blanks and can reduce productivity by up to 40%.[3]

And the bad news continues. As well as slowing you down, it appears that doing more than one thing at a time may actually dumb you down. A study from the University of London found that participants who multi-tasked experienced IQ declines similar to smoking marijuana or staying up all night. In fact, IQ declines for men who multi-tasked placed them in the intellectual range of an eight-year-old child.[4] (And women, don't think you are immune to this effect!)

If the risks of being less productive and intelligent don't motivate you, brains can be damaged in other ways by doing too much at once. MRI scans of people who spend time on multiple devices (think watching TV while scrolling on your iPad) revealed less brain density in the anterior cingulate cortex. This is the area in the brain responsible for empathy, cognitive and emotional control. Further, the area of the brain responsible for positive emotions takes a battering when you are thinking about too many things at once, which might explain why juggling a massive to-do list rarely rates as an activity that brings great joy to someone's life![5]

Mindless mistakes, fraying relationships, inattentive service, exhausted parents and stressed-out workers are the inevitable results of trying to do too much at once. When you focus on the person in front of you, giving them the precious gift of full attention, not only do you strengthen your relationship, you hear more and learn more. When you attend to one challenge at a time, you bring your full resources of mind to bear and that's bound to lead to a better result. A single point of focus will boost your productivity and performance, while at the same time enhancing well-being and happiness.

+ How strong is your multi-tasking habit?

Let's see if your multi-tasking habit is affecting you. Do you regularly experience any of the following?

- ☐ Feeling aimless
- ☐ Feeling restless
- ☐ Being reckless or impulsive
- ☐ Losing self-discipline and control
- ☐ Being tactless or insensitive
- ☐ Unable to think creatively
- ☐ Doing things on autopilot, not noticing that the way you do it needs to change
- ☐ Struggling to finish things
- ☐ Feeling apathetic or indifferent
- ☐ Failing to realise the consequences of your actions
- ☐ Lacking spontaneity
- ☐ Losing interest in something quickly
- ☐ Unable to sustain focused attention
- ☐ Being absentminded
- ☐ Unable to plan ahead
- ☐ Showing lack of concern about things

These are all symptoms of prefrontal cortex damage. Even without an injury, you can experience similar symptoms when multi-tasking puts your brain under too much pressure. Don't worry, this exercise will help you recover its power.

+ Try this . . . Pay full price

We've all heard the command: *Pay attention!* Attention really is a currency that you exchange to get something back: awareness, understanding or connection. When you fail to give full attention because you are multi-tasking or allowing distractions to intrude, you are just short-changing yourself and others. Instead, experiment with paying full price.

Pick one of the following tasks and make a commitment, when it arises in your day, to **pay full price**:

- ☐ Walking or exercising
- ☐ Speaking on the phone
- ☐ Preparing a meal
- ☐ Driving the car

This means that you consciously set aside any other tasks and just do this one with complete attention. When you are on the phone, be fully present with the other person and resist the urge to continue tapping on your computer, watching TV, or walking around the house putting things away. Even more than this, stay focused on the dialogue, instead of letting your mind drift to things like planning what you are going to do once you get off the phone. If you are preparing a meal, stay present with the food and the process you are undertaking. Don't try to coordinate the homework efforts, make phone calls or worry about what the day may hold. When you are walking or exercising, be fully aware of the movements of your body and notice your surroundings. Don't listen to music, make a phone call, or mentally toss around your work problems. When you are driving the car, keep the music off and resist making phone calls. Just be aware of the flow of the traffic and your place in it.

If you get interrupted during any of your chosen tasks, be aware of the moment when you are tempted to multi-task and instead choose wisely, whether you switch your attention to the new task or stay with your chosen task. Remember, the goal of this exercise is to **pay full price to one task at a time**, as a way of breaking the multi-tasking habit.

A good way to maintain a high quality of focus is to imagine you are striving for excellence. Drive like you are taking a test for your licence; cook like you are a contestant on a TV show; listen like you will be tested on what you have just heard; and move like you are on the catwalk!

Initially, you'll probably worry that you won't get enough done, or maybe that you will be bored. But in fact, you may be surprised by how productive and re-energised you feel when you pay full price. And it's something you can do in any task at any time, so don't hesitate to extend it to other things you do in your day.

Supermum rose to the challenge and, despite the first couple of hours in her day being the busiest, she decided to pay full price to each activity that made up her morning. 'I made a conscious choice to do each and every task in the morning like it was a meditation. When I was drinking my tea, I was simply drinking my tea. When I was pouring the porridge, I was simply pouring the porridge. And here's the astounding thing. Not only did I get through everything just as quickly, I was relaxed and my kids were relaxed. It was no longer the chaotic start to the day it used to be for all of us!'

−+ −+

When you realise nothing is lacking,
the whole world belongs to you.

−+ −+

Lao Tzu,
philosopher from Ancient China

Exercise 2
Date Yourself

-+ -+

Being alone gives you the chance to find the best in yourself.

When was the last time you sat alone with your own thoughts? Not sitting at a cafe playing on a device, or zoning out in front of the TV, but simply sitting and enjoying your own company with no distractions. It almost seems like all the ways we used to do this have become old-fashioned: rocking in a hammock, looking out the window, people watching, going for a walk without headphones. So many of these simple actions have lost their place in a normal day, or have been relegated to holidays.

Solitude offers great opportunity to reflect and to connect with your own deeper wisdom. Being without the distraction of another person means you can hear your own voice more clearly. But if you haven't spent time alone lately, or if you fill the time that you are alone with distraction, noise and busy activity, you may feel a natural resistance to trying it. Too many people fill their day with activity, stay in relationships that aren't meeting their needs, and overschedule their calendars just to avoid meeting themselves.

'Anyone up for drinks on Friday night?' He was a busy boy and a social coordinator extraordinaire. His weekends were full and he looked uncomfortable even leaving the office to buy his lunch. He played sport three nights a week and never spent any nights at home alone. 'Go out alone?' He looked horrified at the thought. 'People will think I'm some sort of loser!' But what he didn't realise was that most people saw his constant need for entertainment as a mask for something deeper.

Sure, some people are natural extroverts, drawing energy from being engaged with as many people and as much activity as possible. But no matter where you sit on the introversion-extroversion scale, this exercise is about ensuring that you can embrace time spent with yourself, no matter how often it occurs.

The relationship you have with yourself is the most important relationship you will ever have. Feeling comfortable there takes practice, just as it does to build a relationship with anyone else. Avoiding yourself (either intentionally or unintentionally) because it makes you uncomfortable is ultimately counterproductive. Rather than fearing what you may find, consider instead the rich resources just waiting to be unearthed. The chatter of negative thoughts is generally only skin deep, and it is only made louder by skimming across the surface of life. If you allow yourself to be alone as a positive and purposeful activity, you can reach a more relaxed and contemplative state where the loyal and compassionate voice of intuition and inner guidance offers its support.

The good news is that being alone gets easier with practice. Like any habit, the more you do it the more comfortable you will feel.

+ Can you be alone?

This quiz will give you an insight into how well you use your alone time. Read each question then circle the answer that best describes how you would react.

Question 1: The thought of a night alone at home:
    A. Excites me
    B. Scares me
    C. Is fine—but I will need something to do or someone to call

Question 2: You arrive thirty minutes early at a cafe where you are meeting a friend. While waiting there for the thirty minutes, you are more likely to feel:
    A. Relaxed
    B. Uncomfortable
    C. Fine—but that's because I would find something to do

Question 3: While you're waiting at this cafe for thirty minutes, you would be more likely to:
    A. Relax, sit back and enjoy the opportunity to take a breather

B. Get out your phone or a piece of paper and start doing something useful

C. Take the opportunity to do something creative or contemplative that you never get around to doing

Question 4: You have unexpectedly been given the day off. You are most likely to:

A. Embrace the freedom and indulge in generally doing nothing all day

B. Fill it with tasks that you've been trying to tick off the list for a while

C. Plan a couple of nice things to do and also allow some space for seeing what arises

If you had more As:
you are comfortable with doing nothing and spending time with yourself.

If you had more Bs:
being alone feels uncomfortable and sometimes scary, so it's time to bite the bullet and meet yourself.

If you had more Cs:
there is opportunity to deepen your experiences of being alone.

+ Try this . . . Date yourself

This week take yourself out on a date. It could be for a coffee, meal or outing in the park. Schedule the date like an appointment in your diary, so you don't lose the time to other things. Decide where, when and all the relevant details as if you were inviting a friend. During the whole time that you spend on this date, disconnect from technology and resist the temptation to 'do' something. Simply be alone with yourself and your own thoughts. No to-do lists, no planning, no checking phones.

Notice any discomfort or thoughts that arise. It may happen because you think everyone is looking at you, but they're probably too busy to spare you a second glance! Or you may feel that gnawing sense that you should be doing something else. Just remember there is great purpose to this activity, and you are where you need to be right now.

See if you can reach the delicious point where your body starts to relax, your breathing slows, you feel content in the moment, and the wonder of your own thoughts provides entertainment enough.

-+ -+

I wish that life should not be cheap,
but sacred. I wish the days to be
as centuries, loaded, fragrant.

-+ -+

Ralph Waldo Emerson,
American essayist and poet

Exercise 3
Sounds of Silence

-+ -+

Silence is golden.

S tanding high on the mountain, the silence was deafening. 'I don't think I have ever heard complete silence before,' she remarked to her husband. They both noticed the calming effect it had on them almost instantaneously. But the silence experienced on that weekend away was a far cry from their life in the big city. Stressed out, overwhelmed and constantly assaulted by a barrage of noise coming at them from all directions was their daily norm. 'Maybe we need to go away once a month,' he suggested. 'Maybe we need to find some silence in our busy lives,' she replied.

Most of us are exposed to constant noise. It might only be subtle and therefore often overlooked. But consider your work and home spaces:

☐ Is the radio often playing in the background?

☐ Does the TV get turned on in the morning or evening and left running, even when no-one is watching?

☐ Is there traffic noise, air conditioning, ventilation fans, planes flying overhead, or the hum of other human busyness in the distance?

All of this white noise can hold you back from fully settling into the nourishing folds of empty space.

Hearing is your second most dominant sense after sight, and much of your awareness of your surroundings enters via the ears. This also means that your attention is quite easily distracted by sounds. People who work in open plan offices regularly report that their greatest source of frustration is the distraction caused by the sound of other people talking or laughing. So it makes sense that noise will intrude on any efforts to reflect deeply or access creative ideas and wise insights, as these rely on relaxed and unharnessed attention. Of course, it's not possible to find complete silence, unless you travel out to a remote desert! The sort of silence we're talking about discovering in day to day life will still be full of sounds, but if you can eliminate the layers of unnecessary noise, you will find there is a place where the background sounds are not distracting or agitating, but are instead life's natural sound-track.

Vipassana is one of India's most ancient meditation techniques, in which participants spend ten days or more in silence. Vipassana means 'to see things as they really are.' When you enjoy periods of silence, your ability to self-reflect, observe sensations and understand your thought patterns become stronger. You become more aware of what is driving your behaviour.

A 2013 study of mice found that, when they were exposed to just two hours of silence per day, new cells developed in the hippocampus. This brain region is associated with memory, learning and emotion. These studies seem to suggest that silence doesn't only help you feel more at peace and develop deeper self-awareness, it is also essential if you want a healthy brain.[1]

You will have experienced the benefits of silence at times in your life, but maybe not realised that this warm blanket held such rewards. Often your best thinking comes not from analysis and problem-solving, but in the silence when you lift your head and stop trying. Perhaps in the moment before you drifted off to sleep, you remembered something important that you meant to do. Or, as you admired the beauty of a sunset, a problem that had been bothering you was instantly solved.

How would your life be different if you lived by the philosophy that an important way to find answers is not to fill your mind with the noise of other opinions and more information, but to remove yourself from it all and let the silence weave its magic? What if you accepted that your knowledge and wisdom can grow healthy by exposing yourself not to podcasts, TV shows and webinars, but to the glorious sounds of silence?

You don't need to jump straight into ten days of meditation to embrace silence. And you don't even have to find two hours to reap the benefits. Just begin by finding the places where silence lies waiting in your normal day.

+ Try this ... Sounds of silence

Over the next few days, look for sources of noise in your environment. Are there some that you can reduce or eliminate? Are there alternative places you can go that offer the rare gift of silence? Think about these opportunities:

☐ Instead of listening to music while you walk or run, get rid of the headphones and nourish your mind with the silence of nature.

☐ Turn the radio off when you're in the car.

☐ Resist the temptation to have the TV on while you are doing something else (like reading or eating dinner).

☐ Go to the local library to read or study or work on a project, rather than sitting in a noisy space.

☐ Walk home via a quiet street, rather than the main road.

As you gradually incorporate more silence into your life, picture your memory, learning function and emotional stability growing stronger, and enjoy the gifts of insight and wisdom that emerge when you are not distracted by unnecessary noise.

-+ >

–+ –+

There is more to life than simply increasing its speed.

–+ –+

Mahatma Ghandi,
Hindu political leader and social reformer

Exercise 4
The Pace of Life

-+ -+

Slow is the speed of creation.

S low food, slow travel, slow living . . . everywhere you look there's a slow movement. Sea changing and tree changing have long been popular trends later in life, but today, people aren't waiting for retirement. They are opting in for a dose of 'slow' a lot earlier, exhausted by the ceaseless pace of a modern world and craving a more meaningful connection with life.

If you walk fast, talk fast, finish other people's sentences, dash between meetings, and get frustrated when you're stopped by traffic lights or waiting in a queue, it's time to rediscover the true pace of life.

Modern life races at an unnatural speed. Technology moves fast, responsibilities are many, and there's an expectation of immediate gratification. Your thoughts can move so much faster than your body. So if you live in an 'always on' environment, have an endless to-do list and believe that you can meet every demand, you will always feel like you're in catch-up mode. Rushing, multi-tasking, skipping meals, making snap decisions, cutting conversations off, running late and leaving early are all indicators that you're wound up tight and operating on pure adrenaline. In this state, your brain sprints at full speed like the second hand on a clock face.

When you move too fast, you start missing information and making mistakes. Then you start jumping quickly to conclusions, making assumptions and making poor decisions. You find yourself forgetting things, leaving things behind, spending time on rework and turning up late or not at all. Then you realise you're constantly running through your to-do list, your worries, your deadlines and your responsibilities. At this point you feel like your mind is always three steps ahead of your body. You've forgotten what it feels like to sit back, relax and feel the warmth of the sun, savour a meal or enjoy a conversation.

Few of life's rich and important experiences unfold at this speed. In fact, it's almost impossible to bring your body and your brain back together until you dial it down.

Slowing down is the key to rest, recovery and replenishing your energy. Slowing down is the recipe for caring, connecting and relating to others. Slowing down is the only way to experience beauty, to learn something new, and to become comfortable in your own skin. Your fast-moving mind makes your body move fast, but slowing down your body can help to slow your mind.

Human beings evolved to operate most effectively when we are in tune with the pace of nature. The swaying branches of a large tree, the ebb and flow of the tides, the movement of the sun across the sky—each of these natural rhythms offers a lesson in how to get back in tune with yourself. The frequency of your brainwaves changes when you slow down, reflecting the deeper and more complex connections responsible for moments of insight and deeply-satisfying experiences. But if you can't slow down, these rewards remain out of reach.

'He is like a whirlwind, but in a completely chaotic way.' The group of staff was sitting around talking about their leader. 'He is always racing from one thing to the next. He talks at a hundred miles an hour, and you never get just one email from him, you get ten at a time. He doesn't seem to realise that, while he might think he's being efficient, he leaves destruction in his path. We feel anxious just being near him.'

While it's easy to get dragged along by the frantic 'action addicts' who whisk through our lives, those who move gracefully, think in a considered manner, and portray a calm disposition bring a desirable steadiness to us all.

+ What's your pace?

Ask yourself the following questions. Just let a 'yes' or a 'no' arise, as soon as you read each one:

☐ Do you recall noticing the taste and textures of your last meal?

☐ Do you recall noticing the feel of different ground surfaces under your feet as you walked today?

☐ Think of one person you interacted with today who you see often. Did you notice anything different about them today?

☐ When you've been forced to stop and wait for something today, did you lift your head and just enjoy the moment?

☐ Before reading this question, had you noticed any discomfort in your body today?

☐ Did you learn anything new today?

☐ Have you deviated from your plans today to do something nice for yourself?

If you answered 'no' to many of these questions, you are probably moving too fast. We invite you to get in tune with life's natural pace and discover the gems that can only be seen when you slow down.

+ Try this . . . The pace of life

At least five times a day, slow your movements down to half your normal speed. Try some of these suggestions:

☐ Walk more slowly from place to place. Notice how you naturally lift your head and become aware of your surroundings when you move more slowly. You may also find that slowing down improves your posture.

☐ Slow down your conversations. Try slowing your speech, and you can also try listening more patiently to the other person's response. You'll probably learn a lot more than you thought you would.

☐ In any task, move your body more slowly than normal. As you pick items up, feel their texture; as you put them down, place them gently. As you drive a car, be more conscious of feeling the steering wheel, changing the gears gently, and feeling your foot on the brake.

☐ Eat more slowly than you normally would. You'll probably become more aware of tastes and textures, and may even enjoy the meal!

☐ Take more time in your 'hellos' and 'goodbyes' to loved ones. Try a seven-second hug, real eye contact, and wave them off until they are out of sight.

Initially it will be difficult to slow down, but the rewards are great. So persevere!

When the staff were asked for feedback on their leader a few months after he started his leadership program, the story was quite different. 'You know I think he has only really changed one thing. He doesn't tear around the office corridors anymore. He seems more relaxed and walks slowly between meetings. He also stops by and asks questions about the work we are doing. I feel a lot more supported by him.'

-+ -+

People should not consider so much what they are to *do*, as what they *are*.

-+ -+

Meister Eckhart,
German theologian and philosopher

Exercise 5
The 'Not to Do' List

-+ -+

The value of your life is defined more by the things you choose not to do.

When you wake up, is your first thought: *What day is it and what do I need to get done today?* Do you formulate a long to-do list before your feet even hit the floor? I bet that's not where it ends. You probably run through it again in the shower, add things to it while you're getting ready, and feel like it's your constant companion whispering unwelcome reminders in your ear all day.

There's nothing wrong with having a to-do list. They are useful tools to remind you of necessary activities and, if you use them correctly, they should help to keep your head clear. But it seems like they're having the opposite effect. 'Doing things' carries the addictive potential of a hard drug. The dopamine hit from crossing a task off your to-do list can be deeply satisfying, even if the thing on your list held no importance. It's easy to see why it's so tempting to keep adding things to the list and why it's so distressing when things sit there unfinished. When the to-do list starts dictating your day and defining your self-worth, you eventually feel like a mouse on a treadmill, working hard but getting nowhere.

'I always clear out my email inbox before I leave for the day. I make sure I action every single email and then leave with an empty inbox. It sets me up right for the next day.' Not only was he falling for his brain's trap of finding satisfaction in action, but this habit was also cutting into his time with family. It was not until he decided to take a closer look at what he was doing that he also noticed how many of the emails he sent during this time were unnecessary. Either he was responding when there was no need, asking someone else to take action prematurely, or creating more work for himself the next day. By removing this task off his to-do list at the end of each day, he also relieved much of the pressure he had been putting himself under when he was already tired.

To-do lists are only helpful tools when you also know what **not** to put on them. If you don't have a discerning approach to each item before your add it, your list will inevitably grow and grow. It will get too long to be humanly possible to complete; it will cause great frustration when the day you had planned is not the day that unfolds; and it will drive you to undertake tasks that didn't need to be done.

Recently our friends moved out of their home because the coming year would take them to four different locations for a few months each time. Not only did they have the enormous task of selling all their possessions and moving out of their apartment, they also had to plan the trip to their first location. As you can imagine, this could easily have turned into pages and pages of to-do lists, and they definitely had a few of them! But one of them explained how they were also really conscious of how much her mind wanted to jump forward and start bedding things down for later stages of the year.

'I would think of something like: *Where's the best suburb to rent if I need to travel from the airport every week?* Problem was, those stages were still flexible and depended on a few other things happening before I would know enough to plan them. Rather than legitimising their call for attention by adding them to my to-do list when they actually did not need to be done, and rather than letting them circle in my mind as loose ends, I wrote them on a 'not to-do list'. It was really wonderful to be able to recognise them for what they were—to consciously park them, saving precious time and energy for the things that were real needs and valued achievements.'

+ Try this: . . . The 'not to do' list

Start by writing a comprehensive list of all the things you believe you must do over the next 24 hours. Include work tasks and general life tasks, and any little ideas that have been making you think: *Maybe I should do something about that.* As well as capturing all the physical tasks, consider the things that are occupying your mental space and list those too. For example, worrying about how you're going to get three kids to different sporting events next weekend if it rains.

Now go through each item and use the following questions to help you decide if the item really belongs on your to-do list or not:

- ☐ Does this activity need to be done now?
- ☐ Can I identify a real need that this activity will fulfil?
- ☐ Is this activity ready to be actioned, or does something more need to unfold first?
- ☐ Is this activity truly a stepping stone to the outcome I'm seeking, or could it end up being a waste of time or irrelevant?
- ☐ Does this activity deliver the right amount of value for the effort that will be required?
- ☐ Is this an activity that is mine to do, or am I taking on something that belongs to someone else?
- ☐ Will this activity make a difference to something meaningful, or will I just get a fleeting reward from ticking it off?
- ☐ If this activity is something I'm taking on by choice, will it bring me joy or take me closer to something I genuinely care about?

Have you found some items can be transferred to your 'not to do' list? If so, actually write them down under the heading "Not to do" just as you would write a to-do list. It's your choice and no-one else can tell you where things belong. But simply asking yourself those questions and having an option to put things on a different list can be very liberating.

Each morning, as you consider your day ahead and run through your to-do list, also write yourself a 'not to do' list. Aim to put at least three things on it each day, and include all the things you are choosing to **not** spend time thinking about on that day. As you feel space returning to your life, resist the temptation to fill it with more things to do; instead allow novel, joyful and inspiring things to arise.

-+ -+

Drink your tea slowly and reverently,
as if it is the axis on which the world
earth revolves—slowly, evenly, without
rushing toward the future. Live the actual
moment. Only this moment is life.

-+ -+

Thich Nhat Hanh,
Vietnamese Buddhist monk and peace activist

Exercise 6
Space Day

-+ -+

Space allows you to see life's true plan.

'So what exciting plans do you have for your business next year?' our old friend asked enthusiastically.

'No real plans.'

Our response seemed to leave her at a loss. 'Sorry, you've got no plans? Ooh . . .'

Everyone feels a bit more comfortable when there's a plan in place. Creating a plan and executing the plan satisfies the brain's need for certainty and control; not having one can generate fear and doubt. It's like you're saying 'I don't know what to do,' or 'I'm not going to do anything.' But the truth is, you will. People with purpose and a passion for bringing their best to the world will always be active, but a plan is no guarantee that you will be active on what matters most. Allowing space to see what genuinely unfolds and how you can truly make a difference to the world will be far more effective, and far more satisfying.

When we saw the same friend a year later, her enthusiasm was again on display. 'What a year you've had! Another book, sold-out workshops, the award for your leadership program. Things just seem to happen for you guys!'

The most productive and creative people work with the flow of energy that's unfolding around them. If the energy isn't there, they aren't afraid to change course or stop taking action. When your activity is driven by the plan in your head instead of life's true plan as it unfolds in front of you, it will often be difficult, frustrating, exhausting and ineffectual.

We recently watched the journey of an entrepreneur who decided to launch a major festival. It sounded like a great idea on paper, but as she shared her experiences of trying to get it off the ground in her regular blog, it became clear that the effort she was putting in was not reaping the return she had hoped. After months of sleepless nights, tiring travel, tens of thousands of dollars invested, and hard core hustle to attract performers, sponsors and an audience, the festival folded at the final hour. There was no doubt she had given her all in her attempt to bring this idea to life, and she had followed all the right strategies you would normally see in a successful event, but the signs that things were not falling into place were there all the way along and she failed to see them.

Being able to see this resistance and adapt your plan, rather than always pushing through, requires space to listen to both the messages the world is trying to send you and also your own intuition. The brain has a tendency to want to keep moving forward to finish things, and many people have a personality preference that values structure and planning. But even if you lean this way, allowing yourself the space to recognise when it's time to stop or change your direction is essential.

Now we're not saying that planning is worthless, or that effort is not required. We make plans regularly, but the only thing that remains fixed in our plans is that we strive to always be true to our purpose. Our assumptions, goals and tactics can change, and they inevitably do. And we work hard; but we've learnt to recognise the difference between working in tune with things that have momentum, and paddling against the stream and getting nowhere. We don't always get it right, but you become much more attuned to the signs when you give yourself the space to notice them.

When the things that you do are in concert with the flow of the world and meet the needs that are emerging before you, they are likely to be embraced without struggle. If a door's too hard to open, maybe it's not the right door. If the strategy in your plan is not producing an outcome, maybe you're looking in the wrong place. But unless you leave space to adapt, let go and consider a different direction, you will miss all the opportunities that lie in wait for you.

Certainly working with the plan that is unfolding around you is not as easy as it may sound. It requires patience. Things unfold in their own time, and rarely at the time you'd planned. Sometimes they are faster, sometimes much slower. The type of thinking you use when planning is quite rational, linear and predictable, but life's not like that. Which is why claiming space to let your mind release this type of thinking and connect with rhythms that can only be sensed by your more intuitive and perceptive self is crucial.

Is there an area of your life that's hard work, where you're struggling to move forward and feel like you are paddling against the stream? Can you remember times when you experienced the opposite, and felt like you were moving with the stream, propelled forward with little effort?

+ Do you push or do you flow?

Circle your response to the following questions:

Would you describe the process of 'getting things done' in your life as often:

        A. Hard

        B. Easy

What do you pay more attention to?

        A. The plan you have in your head

        B. Responding to what's unfolding in front of you

Do you find yourself more often:

        A. Pushing

        B. Allowing

When something doesn't work, do you find yourself:

        A. Trying harder

        B. Adjusting your plan to find an easier way

Would you prefer to:
>   A.   Perfect an idea or plan, then execute it
>   B.   Start with the nub of an idea, then throw it into the world and experiment

What happens more often to you?
>   A.   Obstacles arise in front of me
>   B.   Doors open in front of me

Do you more regularly experience:
>   A.   Bad luck situations that make it even harder to get where you want to go
>   B.   Lucky synchronicities that make life easy

If your answers were predominantly As, it sounds like you're more likely to push towards the actions you have planned in your head, and probably feel a bit out of control if you don't have a plan to follow. You will find the Space day uncomfortable, but will benefit greatly from letting go of control and connecting with guidance that is more subtle.

If your answers were predominantly Bs, it sounds like you are more comfortable going with the flow, and already know there is value in being prepared to go 'off plan' if the signs suggest it is necessary. You can use the Space day to perfect the art further.

+ Try this . . . Space day
Schedule yourself a Space day. This is a day without appointments, commitments, meetings or obligations. On

your Space day, work with what unfolds around you and resist making a plan. It means you will need to take the time to observe, notice and, most importantly, sense where the energy of the day is flowing.

This may result in very simple experiences, like going into a shop you would normally walk straight past; or stopping to help a stranger rather than rushing to a meeting; or running into someone and finally having the opportunity to sit down with them and hear a new perspective. A Space day may also allow you to look into something that fascinates you, or follow an idea that you hadn't considered before.

Start your Space day slowly and allow your body to be relaxed. Remember, you have nowhere to be and nothing you must do. Seek to enjoy your morning routines and find a sense of freedom. At the right time for you, when you feel that your Task Positive Network has released its grip and your deeper intuitive self is ready to be heard, close your eyes, put your hand on your heart and slowly ask yourself any or all of these questions:

- ☐ What is here for me today?
- ☐ What does my body need to feel inspired?
- ☐ What do I have energy for today?
- ☐ Where am I being invited to wander today?
- ☐ How can I be of service today?

Once you have an answer, follow the energy and follow the inspiration. Don't try to predict where it will lead, and continue to take your signals about what to do next from what actually happens, not by returning to a plan in your head. Whenever the 'shoulds' and 'musts' try to return to your mind, take a deep breath and remind yourself that today is your Space day and all the other things can wait until tomorrow.

−+ −+

The most important thing is to enjoy your
life—to be happy—it's all that matters.

−+ −+

Audrey Hepburn,
film and fashion icon

Exercise 7
The Working Hours Diet

-+ -+

Focusing on what really matters is what really matters.

I'll have some downtime with the kids when I get through everything I have to do today.'

'I'll call you for a coffee when things slow down a bit.'

'I'd love to make that recipe. Maybe I'll have some time this weekend.'

No doubt you have heard promises like this before, and chances are you have said something similar yourself. If so, you also know that getting through everything rarely happens, and the hoped for downtime, me-time or family time never materialises.

Despite the worldwide trend of increasing working hours, the fact is that working any longer than the traditional 40-hour working week is a sure way to **lower** your productivity and effectiveness. From as far back as the early 1900s, studies have repeatedly shown that worker productivity improves when working hours are reduced from sixty to forty hours a week. In fact, researchers at Stanford University have been unable to find any studies showing that extending work hours delivers higher output in any field.[1] When it comes to achieving outcomes, more is not better.

Keeping your work hours contained makes sense for a few reasons. It leaves enough time in the week to get non-work things done, and this is important. If you haven't got time to do the shopping, help the kids with their homework, fit in some exercise, research your next holiday and grab a lunch with a close friend, then happiness declines, stress rises and your motivation to do your best at work wavers. Life starts to lose its meaning when work dominates at the expense of other things you hold dear—particularly your health, your relationships, and your other interests.

Also, by limiting your working hours you are forced to make choices about what will get done and what won't. Those who know how to say 'no' to requests, who call a stop to something that is not adding value, and who resist the allure of distractions, are the people who get most done.

The truth is, your mental resources are more limited than you may realise. The brain takes a lot of energy from the body to conduct its many complex activities during the day. The most productive people tend to undertake deep attention work (which refers to the tasks that need undistracted focus and access to your best mental resources) for no more than four to five hours per day—and that's the most productive people! The rest of their work hours are filled with light tasks that require less intense concentration, or valued periods of contemplation and curious exploration.[2]

So working longer hours simply doesn't make sense. It will also make you vulnerable to health problems. An analysis of 25 studies collecting data from more than 600,000 people in Australia, the US and Europe for up to 8.5 years, found that people who worked 55 hours a week had a 33% greater risk of having a stroke than people who worked a 35 to 40-hour week.[3]

Yet still people fall for the trap of believing that working longer increases output. A recent Australian study of full-time workers who are paid for an official working week of 38 hours, found that 65% of these workers put in more than 40 hours, and nearly 30% put in more than 50 hours. An 'elite' 1% put in more than 70 hours per week![4]

If you pride yourself on your long working hours, you may want to consider if all the time and effort you are putting in really goes to things that matter. Adding more hours to the working day often means doing tasks just because they arise and not because they are worthwhile or even ultimately necessary. And every hour you add to the working day takes time away from things that matter to the rest of your life. An extra hour every day for just one week means five hours less spent with family, friends, or on your own personal health and happiness.

When you have less hours to get things done, you are more likely to focus on what really matters. And then you also have time for the rest of your life, and that matters too.

+ What really matters most?

Grab a piece of paper and a pen, and draw a line down the middle of the page, so you have two columns. In the left column write down three to five things that really matter to you, the things you believe deserve your best quality attention. Now in the right column list three to five things that get most of your attention in any given day or week.

Compare the lists. How do they measure up? If you are like most people, you will see that your attention is often stolen away from the things that matter most.

When redressing this imbalance, it's easy to fall into the trap of broken promises and *I'll get to that when . . .* , but until you create space and force a limitation on distractions, expectations and short-term pressures, you will struggle to beat them.

+ Try this . . . The working hours diet

Whether you work for someone else, are self-employed, or consider your work to be a combination of activities you do around the home or elsewhere, consider these questions:

- ☐ How many hours do you spend working each day?
- ☐ How much time do you work above and beyond the hours officially defined by your employer (if relevant)?
- ☐ How many of your working hours would you actually consider to be truly productive?
- ☐ If you reduced your working time by one hour each day, what would you stop doing?

So give it a try. For one week, put yourself on a working hours 'diet'. From whatever your baseline is, set yourself a limit of hours for the week which is at least five hours less than you normally dedicate to that work. It may sound like a lot, but until you really experiment with the counter-intuitive nature of getting more done by dedicating less time, you will not realise how powerful it can be. Sweden is experimenting with a six-hour working day, and many employees did not initially believe this was possible for them. But once they tried it, they found that they had fewer meetings, avoided distractions such as social media, sick leave levels fell, and the quality of work was higher.[5]

Throughout the week, notice what this limitation forces you to stop doing. Maybe you will find the discipline to say 'no' to something you would normally agree to. Maybe you will stop taking work home and letting it eat into family time. Maybe you will change your priorities and get the deep work done first. Maybe you will spend less time perfecting something and keep it moving, so you can get to the next task sooner.

Notice any temptation to add to your working hours and, at least for this week, resist it. The working hours diet will make you more conscious of your choices, improve your impulse control, and reward you with more opportunities to indulge in life's wider experiences.

-+ -+

Everyone has inside them a piece of
good news. The good news is that you
don't know how great you can be! How
much you can love! What you can
accomplish! And what your potential is!

-+ -+

Anne Frank,
German-born diarist

Exercise 8
Intuition Booster

-+ -+

Your intuition is the keeper of secrets that your brain doesn't quite yet understand.

I ntuition is an underrated decision-making and guidance tool. Whether you call it gut feel, the voice within, or instinct, there is a very subtle knowledge that resides in us all.

I just knew that would happen.
I had a funny feeling about this from the start.
This doesn't feel right.

You know the feeling, and you probably also know the frustration you feel when you realise you should have listened. The problem is that the voice within that whispers its quiet message is generally immediately followed by the voice in your brain that starts analysing it all. For most of us, this voice is louder and logical, so it's much easier to justify its conclusions and act on those.

Your body is an extraordinary source of truth. If there is a path you should avoid, you'll quickly be alerted by that feeling in your stomach. And if you want to know the answer to your life purpose, don't try to work it out in your head. Your body will show you by deeply relaxing, bubbling with joy or simply feeling content and at home.

Intuition is often dismissed as New Age or mystical, because it can be so difficult to explain the reason for a reaction in any rational way. This is because the intuitive system knows the answers long before the rational one does.

Many studies have revealed that trusting your intuition can often lead to better outcomes than relying on your slower rational brain. In one of these studies, car buyers were divided into two groups. One group was given time to pour over specifications and information before analysing their car choices. The other group made a quick instinctive decision. Those who relied on their intuition were satisfied with their purchase 60% of the time, compared with 25% for those who spent time analysing the information.[1]

Other studies suggest that intuition is unreliable, and that people can make mistakes by relying on 'gut feel'. The truth is that what many people attribute to intuition may not be that at all. We can all get captured by group-think, biases, assumptions, the random thoughts generated in a busy mind, or even learned responses. *I don't have a good feeling about this* could be intuition, but it may also be a response to a similar situation that you did not enjoy once before. A thought is not necessarily an insight, and it takes contemplation and reflection to develop the level of self-awareness necessary to understand the different voices that speak within you.

If your internal world is as busy and distracted as the external one, it is likely that you are not hooking into your intuition very often. Unless you take the time to go inside and connect with your inner self, the voice will get weaker. If you rarely hear it, this means your guidance is mostly coming from your rational processes, which fall regularly into the trap of missing things, focusing on threats, following patterns, and underrating emotional factors. Too often the brain's voice that focuses on warning, worrying and withdrawing overrules your intuition's voice that presents possibility and potential.

Tapping into your intuition takes regular exercise. Being prepared to hear the voice is your first challenge, and this means leaving space and stillness to allow that quiet whisper to be heard. Because the intuitive system relies not only on the brain, but operates via a connection between your body, your emotions and your neural activity, it is essential to let yourself be relaxed and in tune with the way you **feel**, rather than the way you **think**.

It is also essential to strengthen your faith in its messages. Rather than allowing your brain to jump straight into the game of second-guessing everything you feel, build the confidence to act on your intuition. Over time, you will realise how reliable your intuition can be.

Next time you are searching for an expert to tell you what to do, how to react and what to believe, turn to the one inside.

+ Try this ... Intuition booster

Tap in daily to your inner voice. Place your hands on your stomach, take a few deep breaths and imagine yourself going deep, deep inside to seek counsel with yourself. Take two minutes to let go of the grip being held by your brain's voice, and allow your awareness to settle fully into your body.

Ask yourself these questions:

☐ How am I feeling right now?

☐ What do I need today to feel happy, alive and connected?

Then think of a question you'd like the answer to at that moment, and simply ask it.

The answer could come in words, a symbol or a picture, so give up all expectations of what you'll uncover. Don't force an answer and don't search for it. Don't even expect you will always get one. Just simply allow the space for something to appear. If all you can hear is your rational brain chattering away and taking you through logical steps, gently focus back again on your breath, feel your body relax a little more, then try again. Over time, you'll come to know the difference between the two voices.

By practising this exercise regularly, you'll find that you will begin to develop a sense for your gut feel, and you'll notice it without having to always stop to hear it.

-+ >

−+ −+

Be happy in the moment, that's enough.
Each moment is all we need, not more.

−+ −+

Mother Teresa,
Catholic nun and missionary

Exercise 9
The Importance of Being Idle

-+ -+

Idle means 'at rest', and this is something that you need more than you may realise.

ou may not believe it, but you have opportunities to be idle every day. No, we're not talking about lazing around on the couch watching the midday movie, or spending the afternoon surfing the internet watching silly videos while your boss is out of the office. We're talking about opportunities to sit back, lift your head, and let your attention rest. When you miss these opportunities, you're missing an invitation to pass through the doorway to deeper levels of awareness and reflection essential for productivity, meaning and performance.

In decades gone by, stopping for morning tea at work when the tea trolley came around was a common ritual. Everyone in the office would get up, stretch enjoy their cuppa, and chat to their friends or head outside for some fresh air (or not so fresh air for the smokers). No matter what the choice, everyone took their break and detached their minds from the work that had absorbed them for the previous couple of hours. Even after the tea trolley became a thing of the past, we would take breaks to make a cup of tea in the office kitchen or head out to a nearby cafe for a takeaway coffee. We had no mobile devices to bury our heads in while we waited, so we did something other than work: we flicked through the newspaper, chatted with colleagues, or just watched the passing parade of people.

Now when you stand outside a cafe and watch the waiting workers, every head is down and fingers are working fast on screens. The intensity of focus means that their attention has not had its well-deserved break. Even if the focus has switched from work matters to social ones, their attention is still busily chewing through information and skating over the surface of issues, rather than diving deep into the rich ideas waiting below.

'I make sure I have one good holiday each year and that's when I really switch off. Last year we went to a resort where you can't get any internet connection, and it was so great because I read a book, got a massage every day, meditated with the group each morning, and really chilled out.' There were nods around the panel of businesspeople there to discuss how they juggle the perennial work/life balance challenge.

Don't delay your idle time until your annual holiday. Don't even delay it until the weekend. Reclaim the idle moments that appear throughout the day, because they are the moments that reshape your work, redirect your efforts, and renew your focus. Every time you lift your head, your attention is momentarily released from a task and, if you get out of the way and allow it some freedom, it may just reward you with a glimpse of something new, useful, clear and meaningful.

Observe the natural cycles you follow in a day. Do you have micro-moments, when a simple pause to lift your head allows you to find the next step on the path? Do you experience a point in your work when your brain seems to disconnect, and you naturally lift your head? You will have these pauses, but you may never have noticed them. More importantly, notice what you do when they occur. Do you fill the idle moment with something else like checking emails, or do you get out of the way and let your mind settle into a place where it can forage through the amazing resources stored within your brain and offer you a gem?

If you're worried that it's too hard to put idle moments into your life, the good news is that they are already there. The first step is to reclaim the natural gaps that arise. You are bound to have your own idle moments; it's just a matter of peeling back the busyness and rediscovering them.

Some will be micro-moments, like just lifting your head while you're writing an article; waiting for the water in the shower to heat up before you step in; travelling a few floors in an elevator; holding open a door for an elderly customer; or filling your glass of water.

Some will be longer gaps, like taking a bathroom break; making a cup of tea; waiting a few minutes in a meeting room until others arrive; arriving a few minutes early for school pick up; waiting in a line at the supermarket check-out; waiting for a bus; or waiting to cross the road.

Some will be even longer again, like driving between appointments; travelling home on the bus; taking a shower or bath; or sitting on the sidelines watching your kids play sport.

+ What's your idle baseline?

For each of the following situations, consider your normal response. If you tend to fill the gap with activity, put an A (for activity) next to it. If you allow yourself the space to do nothing and be idle in that gap, put an I (for idle) next to it.

What do you do when you:

- ☐ Travel on public transport or drive a car
- ☐ Wait in a queue
- ☐ Arrive early for a gathering
- ☐ Have a break in proceedings at a conference or concert or sporting event
- ☐ Take a coffee break
- ☐ Are in the shower
- ☐ Walk out to lunch or to a meeting across town
- ☐ Finish meeting with someone and are now alone
- ☐ First wake in the morning
- ☐ Take a break from what you are doing for any reason

If there are more As than Is on your list, it's time to reclaim your idle moments.

+ Try this ... The importance of being idle

Identify three opportunities that emerge for you every day that you could reclaim for idling. Maybe it's waiting in the car to pick up the kids, walking between meetings, and waiting for your takeaway coffee.

What are your three?

1. _____

2. _____

3. _____

When these moments arise, say to yourself, 'Idle time is not wasted time.' Then whatever you are doing, lift your head so you are looking out at your environment, let your body be relaxed and open, and move more slowly and intentionally. Become aware of the sounds around you, notice the brightness of the light, and feel the weight of your body sitting in the chair or on the balls of your feet. You don't need to do anything else but this. Your brain will do the rest, so leave it alone!

At the very least, you'll get some moments of rest and recovery during your busy day. But you might get a whole lot more!

Here are some other ways to cultivate idle time in your life:

☐ Try the Pomodoro Method[1], which proposes a five-minute break every thirty minutes and works with the natural flow of your energy. Just be sure not to fill that five minutes with intense activity, and also be careful not to get so distracted that your five-minute break becomes half an hour!

☐ Plan a decent break every season throughout the year. This could just mean enjoying your weekend without any work at all. Or taking a long weekend in the country or at the beach. If you don't take some reasonable doses of rest and recovery regularly, chances are that by the time your annual holiday comes around, you'll be stressed, get sick during the first week off, and won't be able to reach the desired state of relaxation.

-+ >

−+ −+

The voyage of discovery is not in seeking
new landscapes but in having new eyes.

−+ −+

Marcel Proust,
French novelist

Exercise 10
The Beauty of Boredom

-+ -+

Boredom is the birthplace of curiosity.

'I'm bored. Can I play on the iPad?' the eight-year-old asked for the second time that day.

It was only the third day of school holidays and it was one of those times when it would have been easier for mum to say 'yes'. She was tired, had a deadline looming, and an hour's peace and quiet would have been just what she needed. But instead, she packed up a few things and they all headed outside. Miss 10 happily took the sketch pad and pencil and began drawing the beautiful landscape, but Master Eight still wasn't happy. His first attempt at entertaining himself involved disrupting his sister. So then she screamed at him to go away and stop ruining her picture. *You should have brought the iPad for him,* was all mum could think, but she persevered, 'Why don't you go exploring?' After five minutes of gently standing her ground despite his protests, he did just that. Mum opened her notepad and finally found her flow, getting a few really good thoughts down on paper.

'Mummy, do you want to come to my bakery?'

She sighed but quickly corrected herself. 'Yes, sure I do!' she said, as she marched down towards him.

'This is the kitchen, and this is the counter,' said he, happily continuing his game. Soon they were all engrossed in the fun, laughing and imagining together.

Boredom is one of the greatest experiences you can give a child. In fact, it must be experienced during these early years, if they are to have any chance of surviving in a world where their mind is constantly under assault from information, entertainment and distraction. Until faced with the empty space that boredom brings, they have no idea of their creative potential, and they'll never learn how to access it.

Boredom is the birthplace of curiosity. It's in moments after the 'I'm bored' plea from the kids when they'll start investigating something in the backyard, then create a game that entertains them for the rest of the afternoon. But only if you haven't first reacted and made efforts to entertain and distract them.

The same is true for adults. When's the last time you were so bored that you were forced to dip into your creative reserves and come up with something new and novel to entertain or occupy yourself? If you're more likely to grab your mobile device or the newspaper or make a phone call when you're at a loose end, then you're missing out on the beauty of boredom.

Rather than thinking that boredom is a problem to be solved, see it as a positive sign that you are on the road to clearing your mind. Sure, it feels uncomfortable, and that's why people pull out too early. But studies show that an important step before applying yourself to generating creative solutions is to do something mundane and disengaging. It's the study participants who complete the most boring tasks, like reading the phone book, who tend to come up with the most creative ideas[1]. It disengages the busy mind and frees your brain up to access deep and novel connections. Boredom is like a desert you must cross, if you want to reach an oasis of inspiring ideas.

The moment you label something as boring, you tend to reject it. But that doesn't mean it has nothing to offer. Sometimes it's because you know nothing about it that you assume it's boring. Or maybe you know too much about it, and you've become complacent, no longer noticing the things you used to appreciate. Learning to sit with boredom and allow yourself to move to the other side can open up a world of interesting, inspiring and worthwhile experiences.

When was the last time you were bored? Grab a journal or piece of paper and write a short story about it. How did it feel and where did it take you?

For many people, this simple exercise reveals that they haven't felt bored since they were a child. Sure, boring moments arise all the time, but we live in a world where there are just too many opportunities to quickly fill them with ordinary tasks that halt the journey to curiosity in its tracks.

+ Try this ... The beauty of boredom

This exercise offers a few ways to explore the beauty of boredom. The goal is to allow yourself to experience boredom and, rather than backing out of it, settle into it. This gives your curiosity a chance to wake up and discover freshness and vibrancy in the world around you.

Experiment 1   Go to a newsstand and pick out the most boring magazine you can possibly find. It must be something that you have absolutely no interest in. Spend an hour with that as your only companion and resist the urge to pick up a pen or do something else. Just read with full attention.

Experiment 2   Spend time with someone you consider boring. We all have someone we avoid, but avoidance just trains you to run from boredom. Resist the temptation to wind up the conversation or steer it to something that interests you. Just allow your 'boring' mate to take the lead and be fully present with them.

Experiment 3   Examine your reaction to places you visit or pass by: the supermarket, a bus stop, an office foyer, a local park, an art gallery, your own balcony. Whenever you notice that you have labelled a place as 'boring', stop there and take a moment to allow your body and mind to come to rest. Once you are fully present, close your eyes and say to yourself: *See this place with fresh eyes.* Then lift your head and simply observe all aspects of the space as if they are completely new to you. Sometimes 'boring' is just 'familiarity', but a fresh look always finds something new to note.

Keep a journal with you and capture any insights you get during these experiments.

-+ -+

Look deep into nature, and then you
will understand everything better.

-+ -+

Albert Einstein,
theoretical physicist

Exercise *11*
Slice of Nature

-+ -+

*Answers lie in the whispering trees and the soft caress of
the breeze.*

Nothing feels better than a hike up a mountain, a swim
in the ocean or a walk in a rainforest. You feel refreshed
almost immediately, and the calming effect can last for days.
The benefits of time spent in nature are felt by all, and
research now backs this up.

Just a five-minute break in nature can boost performance
in attention and memory tests by 20%. The same results
are not achieved when taking a break to have lunch with
friends or a walk down a city street. And it's not just your
intelligence that benefits. People who spend time in nature
are less likely to suffer from depression and anxiety.[1]

Patting a dog has been proven to lower the stress levels
of owners and, around the world, pets have been introduced
to nursing homes and trauma recovery centres for this very
reason. And nature has many more healing benefits. Next

time you require a stay in hospital, request a window view. Hospital patients with a view of nature from their window heal faster![2]

But despite knowing it is good for us, increasingly busy schedules, the allure of technology, and less downtime cause people in the modern world to lose their connection with nature. Few fully realise the importance of this connection. Not only does it have direct health-boosting and stress-busting benefits, it enhances creativity and cognitive capabilities. Companies are now factoring natural spaces into the design of their buildings, in an attempt to put nature's healing skills to work.

'I have no clarity on what I want to do with my business.' She was sharing her concerns with us just before the leadership workshop was about to kick off.

'Stop thinking about it. You won't work it out in your head.'

After an hour and a half kayaking on the lake at sunrise, she ran up the shore, waving the oars in the air. 'I've got it! I've got my business idea as well as a business plan!' And what an idea it was. She went on to win a business award for new ideas!

All it took was to let her mind fall still and replenish itself in nature. Nature has the power to draw your attention out of your head and into the present. It can generate feelings of awe, and realign your sense of self to feel part of something much greater. All of these experiences correlate well with accessing deeper wisdom and inspiring insights.

Nature is also a remedy for boredom. Once you turn your attention to nature, curiosity is sparked by the complex and magical ways that nature puts things together. It leads your mind towards novel ideas and creative solutions.

Research also reveals that children are healthier, happier, and perhaps even smarter and more creative when they have a connection to nature. Nature has positive effects on children with conditions such as attention deficit disorder, asthma and obesity, and it improves their physical health.[3]

+ What's your favourite slice of nature?

Many traditions recognise four elements of nature. We've added a fifth, based on the research suggesting the power of animals to calm and heal. Which one do you find most grounding and refreshing?

☐ Water—beach, lake, river, rain

☐ Earth—grass, trees, mountains, parks

☐ Air—breeze, sky, clouds, being at heights

☐ Fire—sun, candles, fireplaces

☐ Animals—pets, birds, other wildlife

+ Try this . . . Slice of nature

Think about how you can get a slice of your favourite element in your day, every day. It may need to be a substitute for the 'real thing', but you'll be surprised how it's possible to access something, no matter where you are. Consider raising your face to take in the sun's rays for a few minutes at lunchtime, watching birds flying outside your window, listening to the sounds of a tree gently rustling in a subtle breeze, or feeling the flow of water on your back in the shower.

Every day, spend five minutes connecting with a slice of nature. It might be in your backyard, a small park in your lunchbreak, or the sight of the trees on the way to work. It's important to expose your senses so that your attention is drawn to sights, sounds, touch, tastes and smells of the natural world. So make sure you look up, listen and spend a few moments absorbing it all.

Notice how just a few minutes can clear your mind. Once you achieve a sense of clarity and calm, carry it with you through the rest of the day.

-+ >

−+ −+

The secret of genius is to carry the
spirit of the child into old age.

−+ −+

Aldous Huxley,
English writer and philosopher

Exercise 12
Walk Away and Play

-+ -+

The wisest souls carry a sparkle in their eye.

Play isn't just for fun; it's for learning, for growth and for wisdom. During play, you can experience situations and experiment with ideas in a safe, relaxed and positive environment. When you watch a young child at play, you can see them using their imagination, having loads of ideas, and trying different ways to achieve an outcome. And the fact that it's fun is not just a side benefit. Having fun opens up your brain, making you more likely to engage, to look for positive ways forward, and to remember what you learn.

When we enter adulthood, play often gets left behind. Most workplaces value serious discussions and professional behaviour over fun and frivolity, mistakenly assuming that the former is real work and the latter is just light relief. But from a scientific perspective, the lightness of play has significant effects on how your brain operates. You're likely to be more positive, more imaginative, less inhibited and more engaged with others. While serious problem-solving methods tend to operate within known parameters, play will often shift the boundaries and break down barriers that hold you back from seeing a new approach.[1]

This is not to say that serious problem-solving methods are unimportant. But if you don't develop a comfort with play as one of your options, you could be missing out on lots of brilliant ideas.

'Hey, I've just realised how we could offer our customers a new way to use our services!'

They were engaging in a team-building exercise, following a hard day of business planning. As he explained his idea, heads nodded and more ideas flowed. 'I think we just came up with better solutions in the last thirty minutes than we did through the whole day!' one person said. 'Who'd have thought that climbing ropes would be way more productive than SWOT analysis and scenario planning?!'

The more you play, the better you think. Consider the famous Marshmallow Challenge. Participants are given some dry spaghetti, marshmallows, string and tape, and have fifteen minutes to build a freestanding tower. Replicated many times over, studies of different groups taking on the Challenge reveal surprising results. As you may expect, engineers perform fairly well. What you may not expect is that MBA students perform worst. But the most surprising result is that the highest performers are kindergarten kids![2]

Einstein famously said: *Imagination is everything. It is the preview of life's coming attractions.* Rather than treating play as a guilty pleasure or a luxury to engage in once all the hard work is done, we may do better to recognise it as a legitimate and necessary method for envisioning possible futures, for stepping off well-worn paths, and for accessing our own genius.

+ Try this . . . Walk away and play

When was the last time you had a complex problem to solve? Did you spend hours at your desk researching it to death? Did you analyse it over and over, only to feel like you were getting further away from the solution? Did you toss it around with others only to leave more confused? These are all signs that your serious problem-solving methods have run out of steam. Sounds like it's time to walk away and play!

Here are some ideas for tapping into your playful genius:

☐ Rather than working through lunch, go out with a group of friends who are guaranteed to give you a good laugh. Or instead of staying back in the office as your colleagues head home at the end of the day, call a friend and head out for a friendly game of snooker.

☐ Play a board game with the kids. Let their enthusiasm and out-of-the-box perspective be your guide.

☐ If it's a group problem, take on a team sport challenge: go bowling, play touch football or, if you're stuck in the office, try a trivia quiz! And consider doing the fun stuff before addressing the serious stuff. You might just find the solutions a lot more quickly.

Even if you don't immediately find a solution, when you return to your work you'll find that you've cracked the door open to a fresh perspective and you'll be more motivated to jump in and try again.

-+ >

-+ -+

In today's rush, we all think too much,
seek too much, want too much, and
forget about the joy of just Being.

-+ -+

Eckhart Tolle,
author and spiritual teacher

Exercise *13*
Find Measure

-+ -+

Not too little, not too much, just the perfect dose and the lightest touch.

o you charge through the day only to find yourself exhausted by lunchtime? Are you either 'on' or 'off', with no in-between? Do you find yourself going in circles at a rapid pace, with little to show for it? Do you try so very hard, but feel like the outcome just doesn't match your efforts?

Imagine you have a bucket of energy and attention to use throughout the day. If you pour it out in the first few hours, no wonder there is nothing left to give to things later in the day. And they just might be the things that really matter. Failing to measure out your limited mental and physical resources is a common reason for an afternoon slump, for running out of steam before you get through everything you wanted to do that day, and for falling in a heap when you get home, with barely enough energy left to zone out in front of the TV! While your solution might be to reach for a chocolate bar or a coffee to keep you going, you know that sort of short-term hit is not really solving the problem. In fact it's probably creating a bigger one by causing even greater energy imbalances.

Your activities become more effortless and efficient when you have measure in your day. When you expend an even amount of energy across the day, it allows you to achieve more, be more conscious and intentional about your choices, and be more present for all your tasks. But more importantly, when you match the level of your effort to what is really needed to achieve each task, you will find yourself more satisfied with the outcomes.

Measure is important in all manner of tasks. Even just the simple act of pushing too hard on a knife when cutting bread is a waste of effort. Trying too hard to convince another person of your views, when it's clear they do not agree, is also like pouring precious doses of enthusiasm onto barren soil. Taking on too many appointments and forcing yourself to get to everything that's offered means you're moving too fast to allow any enjoyment to touch you. And thinking through lots of different angles on a problem will take your precious attention away from life as it passes you by.

+ How measured are your efforts?

Circle your responses to the following questions.

Do you find yourself:

A. Exhausted by lunchtime or midafternoon

B. Having stable energy levels throughout
the day

Do you:

A. Start your day fast

B. Ease into the day

When you identify something to be done, do you:

A. Want it done now

B. Consider it in the context of other things
you are doing, and feel comfortable
putting it off, if that looks sensible

Would you describe yourself as:

A. Impatient

B. Patient

After you've achieved something, would you tend to:

A. Move quickly to the next thing

B. Savour the moment, allow yourself time
to refresh, and then consider what you
want to do next

Do you often:

A. Lift your head from your day's activities,
only to find you haven't eaten or looked
after yourself

B. Have awareness of what your body needs
and call a pause to activities, even when
you are busy

If your answers were mainly As, it's time to introduce more measure to your day. You will gain great benefits from slowing down and distributing your bucket of energy more evenly throughout the day.

If your answers were mainly Bs, you are showing signs of being well measured. Your opportunity is to notice what sorts of situations, mindsets or expectations can throw you out of this good habit.

+ Try this . . . Find measure

Dedicate a week to doing everything with 'measure'. This means finding the level at which you can sustain a sense of productivity over the long term. Being measured means putting in the right amount of energy required for a task, nothing more and nothing less. There is a perfect dose of effort for each task, so set yourself the challenge of finding it.

Start with simple physical activities: preparing meals, housework, getting ready to go out in the morning, exercising, typing on a keyboard, and using tools or implements. When you find the perfect measure for each task, you will also feel much more present and connected with it. And you will most likely find that the amount of effort required is a lot less than you had been using.

Once you realise you have the power to adapt your efforts to match different physical activities, move on to other parts of your day. Consider what it means to bring measure to:

☐ Eating and drinking
☐ Different types of work tasks
☐ Conversations and social engagements

☐ Driving a car
☐ Planning for a meeting
☐ Taking on a new project
☐ Sleep habits

The best way to find measure is to pause between each task and check how you're going. Have you been managing your efforts well through the previous task? Are you giving too little or too much? Do you need to slow down and be a little more intentional with the next task? What is the right thing to expend your energy on next?

You know you have achieved measure when you are satisfied with what you have accomplished during a day, you sleep soundly and you can do it all again the next day.

-+ -+

Wanderer, there is no path. You
lay a path in walking.

-+ -+

Antonio Machado,
Spanish poet

Exercise 14
Comfort with Discomfort

-+ -+

If you're not uncomfortable, you're not growing.

M any people would rather suffer the discomfort of a mild electric shock than the discomfort of sitting alone with nothing to do. This tells us a lot about how strange many of our choices can be.

People avoid the void for many reasons: *It's boring. I haven't got time. I don't want to be alone with my thoughts.* All these excuses are different ways of saying the same thing: doing nothing feels uncomfortable. But only until you get used to it.

Think about the last time you were forced to learn a new computer system. You probably had 'brain pain' for the first few days, as your brain tried to create new pathways. It would have been really uncomfortable to change the way your hands moved across that keyboard, and you undoubtedly channelled this discomfort into cursing the software developers! But eventually, after you'd repeated the new method a number of times, it became as habitual as the old method. In fact, you probably quickly forgot how you even did it the old way.

Contrary to popular opinion, discomfort is not something to run from. Discomfort is your brain's way of saying, 'Pay attention, there's something here you need to look at more closely.' When discomfort is a physical thing, you can quickly identify what it wants you to deal with: there's a stone in your shoe and the discomfort makes you stop and take it out. But when it's mental discomfort like frustration, boredom and distaste, it's a little more difficult to interpret, and so the temptation is to move quickly away from the perceived source.

This becomes a real dilemma for those who want to change habits, because changing habits will generate quite pronounced forms of discomfort. The only way to get to the other side and adopt a new habit is to allow, and even embrace, the discomfort that will naturally accompany your new efforts. Otherwise you'll just fall back into a habit you don't like or know is not good for you.

He knew that his habit of taking the iPad to bed with him was unwise. He always stayed up way later than he meant to, watching shows and flicking through work messages, newsfeeds and social media. He knew he wasn't getting enough sleep, because he'd wake up feeling foggy and struggle to stay focused all day at work. His wife had tried to break him out of the habit with all the studies on how bad the light was for his sleep, but he'd downloaded an app to get around that problem. However, if he was honest with himself, he felt bad every night about bringing it to bed, and repeatedly said to himself, 'Next week I'll stop'. But each time he tried, he felt tense, even resentful and a bit angry. All sorts of thoughts would go through his head like: *I've had a big day. I deserve a bit of downtime watching my favourite show!* Then he'd convince himself that just fifteen minutes would be okay. But inevitably fifteen minutes turned into an hour, and he was back in the same place again.

Once your brain has laid down familiar pathways, you tend to repeat habits almost on autopilot. It requires a lot less energy to repeat a habit than it does to try something new and different. So when you go 'off habit', your lazy brain sends all sorts of signals designed to steer you back to the old habit. You'll feel tense, your breathing may become shallow, your pulse increases and you'll feel hyper-alert. You naturally want to pull away from the new behaviour because: *It doesn't feel right* or *I'm no good at that* or *I can't do it* or *I don't want to do it.* But that's not the right interpretation of the message that discomfort is sending you.

Change your relationship with discomfort. Instead of taking it as a sign to give up and retreat back to old habits, you can view discomfort as a positive indicator that you are trying something new. The only way to change, to learn and to grow is to notice your discomfort, accept it and move through it. The discomfort of changing habits can't hurt you, but some of the habits you probably need to change can!

Slowing down and doing less will feel uncomfortable for anyone who has lost the habit, and all that newly-discovered empty space can make the feelings of discomfort more pronounced. But if you change the way you interpret discomfort and use it to measure your progress, you will eventually find a new habit becomes increasingly comfortable each time you repeat it.

+ Try this ... Comfort with discomfort

When was the last time you felt uncomfortable?

- ☐ Today
- ☐ Yesterday
- ☐ Last week
- ☐ Last month
- ☐ Last year
- ☐ Well over a year ago
- ☐ Can't remember

If you haven't been uncomfortable for a while, you might be stuck in a rut! When you change your relationship with discomfort and recognise its positive message,, you'll find it a lot easier to change any habits.

Notice which activities you use to avoid discomfort:

- ☐ Overscheduling your diary, so the moments never arise
- ☐ Researching or planning future events
- ☐ Turning to another task on your to-do list
- ☐ Grabbing a mobile device to check emails, newsfeeds or social media
- ☐ Calling a friend or talking to a colleague
- ☐ Grabbing a snack or a drink
- ☐ Switching on the TV or radio
- ☐ Other?

Now you are forewarned, notice these urges next time you have an idle moment. Instead of using one of these gap fillers to ease the discomfort, just sit or stand in that idle moment and gaze gently out at your environment. Each time you notice signs of discomfort, remind yourself: *This is a positive sign that I am building a new habit. My brain is learning how to slow down and access important new areas.* Consciously release the feelings of discomfort by relaxing your shoulders and slowing your breath, and just let your mind wander for a while.

Do something that makes you feel uncomfortable every day. It might be sitting in the front row at a presentation, speaking up in a group, travelling a different way to work, eating at a new restaurant, or leaving your mobile device at home when you go out. Observe how it feels the first few times you do something new and different, and notice how these feelings change over time. New habits will grow stronger and old habits loosen their grip. Discomfort will fade, and you'll forget why you ever found it so hard!

-+ -+

Perfectionism is a twenty-ton shield that we
lug around thinking it will protect us
when in fact, it's the thing that's really
preventing us from taking flight.

-+ -+

Brené Brown,
American author and public speaker

Exercise 15
Avoid the Perfection Pitfall

-+ -+

Just okay is perfect, if it meets the need.

How much of what is on your plate at the moment did you create for yourself? Don't jump in too quickly to answer the question, but just sit and reflect a while. How often do you go way beyond the call of duty to deliver things that surpass the initial need? And more importantly, what is the cost of this to you?

'I like to do a good job.' She worked twelve-hour days to achieve that.

'She's a great worker, but she could do half of what she does and still be good. Plus I think her staff would respect her more. They find it hard to relate to someone who doesn't have a life.' her boss remarked. 'Leaders who send emails in the middle of the night may think this is showing their commitment, but it puts pressure on their people and it's simply not necessary.'

High performers and perfectionists are different in subtle but important ways. While they both set themselves high standards, high performers match their challenges to their energy. They aim for standards that are relevant and achievable, and they learn something positive from each experience, successful or not. On the other hand, perfectionists impose a set of standards on themselves that are relentlessly high, and ultimately very draining for them. They are driven by their own definition of flawlessness, not by the real need of the situation. They often experience negative self-talk, because it is so difficult for them to achieve success against these expectations. This not only drives them to work harder and longer than may be necessary, it can paralyse them.

The mum of Miss Five was having a hectic time planning her birthday party, frantically searching for the right shade of pink for the napkins, tracking down the princess castle hire, and making the perfect castle cake. When the day came, she was beside herself about the slight lean on the castle cake, and spent ages fussing around it in the kitchen. The other mothers tried repeatedly to tell her it was a wonderful cake, but she couldn't be placated. Of course, when it was carried out to Miss Five and her friends, they squealed excitedly, devoured their pieces, and went straight back to their favourite games. Let's face it, kids don't know the difference between a Martha Stewart production and some flashes of bright colour. Miss Five's happiness was fed by the connection with her friends, and the fun and laughter with her family. Mum's stress levels and disappointment were of her own making.

While perfectionism seems to offer you a sense of being in control (*I like being prepared*), the struggle to meet standards that are beyond the real need of the situation eventually makes you feel out of control (*I'm never going to get this done in time!*).

If your own perfectionist standards are contributing to the busyness in your life, you're sitting on a goldmine. Imagine if you could discover a way to do just what is required to meet the needs of a situation, and not one thing more or one thing less? Not only would you save on the stress, you'd definitely get some time back for more important things, like doing nothing!

+ Do you fit the profile?

People fall into the perfection trap for different reasons. Can you identify yourself in any of these descriptions?

☐ **Martyr**

You don't like delegating or asking for help because you don't think others will do it properly (that is, the way **you** would do it). You know you're overloaded, but you just put your head down and work harder, seeing no other way out. You often complain about your workload, but when someone offers to help, you always find an excuse not to let anything go. On the rare occasion you do let someone else do something, you can't resist changing it all and then you use this as a reason why you'll just do it yourself next time!

☐ People Pleaser

You are the first to volunteer for extra tasks—not because you want the work, but because you want to make people happy. It makes you feel good to receive gratitude, praise and approval. When it comes to delivering a result, this desire to impress means you will often go the extra mile, aiming for a standard worthy of admiration, rather than just doing what needs to be done.

☐ Gold Plater

You like to deliver a Rolls Royce when a Ford was all that was required. You have a clear picture in your mind of how you want things to look or be done, and the thought of delivering less than this perfect picture is not an option for you. You'll search until you find the right part; you'd rather leave something unfinished than take a short cut; and you often miss deadlines because of the difficulty of making the world match your high standards.

The rewards you search for can be found without setting yourself such a high bar. You don't need to drive yourself into the ground to be a valuable member of the team, you don't need to go above and beyond to receive approval, and you don't need to concoct an award-winning design to solve every problem.

The true measure of performance in any area is to meet the real need of the situation. Delivering more can be as inappropriate as delivering less. The challenge for you now is to balance that seesaw, so you achieve not too little, not too much, but 'just right'. That, in fact, would be perfect!

+ Try this ... Avoid the perfection pitfall

Before you dive in and bury yourself in the struggle for perfection, ask yourself these questions:

- ☐ What is the **real need** in this situation?
- ☐ What would a 'just right' solution look like?
- ☐ What solution am I aiming for?
- ☐ If my solution is a higher standard, what's driving that?
- ☐ What benefits can be achieved if I aim for the 'just right' solution, rather than my usual high standards? (Think of the time you'll get back in your day, the energy you can save for something else, your ability to move more quickly to the next task, the satisfaction that the receiver will experience, the deadlines that will be met, and the learning others will receive if you delegate.)

No doubt you will feel very uncomfortable as you navigate around the perfection pitfall. Taking a new path always feels wrong in the beginning, and you will feel a strong pull back to the standards of old. Your brain will try to convince you that your standards are right, and that lowering these standards is a bad thing to do. But remember that your own standards of perfection are not necessarily the standards defined by the real need of the situation. If you can overcome the perfection pitfall, you'll rediscover the lightness of space, the joy of achievement, and a wonderful sense of forward momentum.

-+ -+

It is only by saying 'no' that you
can concentrate on the things
that are really important.

-+ -+

Steve Jobs,
co-founder of Apple Inc.

Exercise 16
The 'No' Note

–+ –+

A 'no' to something is a 'yes' to yourself.

I f you've got a finger in every pie and you're feeling overstretched, you may have difficulty saying 'no'. You probably feel resentful because you are doing too much, but you know there's no-one else to blame for this predicament. Even when you really want to, or know you have to, and even if you have given yourself the pep talk beforehand, you feel the 'yes' slipping through your lips!

'I really need a session with you. Can you meet me at 5:30pm?' It had been a long day and she was looking forward to going home and relaxing. But she agreed. After all, he needed her. She turned up to the session on time, exhausted and ready for a break. He turned up at 5:50pm apologising . . . he had been busy.

You're probably a very agreeable person; a reliable friend who people can turn to; a dedicated worker who is known for getting things done; and a person with a strong sense of responsibility. You don't like to let people down, and you feel guilty when you say 'no' to a request. However you **are** letting someone down. In fact you are letting down the only person who relies on you fully and completely: yourself!

I bet you already have many things to do: things you are passionate about, things that will make you healthier and happier, time you want to spend with family members, priorities that will move your life in the direction you've dreamed of. It's already difficult to embrace your idle moments in a busy life. But when you lease these precious spaces out to other people's requests, you are shuffling yourself to the back of the queue, deferring your dreams, delaying your priorities, and robbing yourself of the precious time you have been given to live a full life.

When you say 'yes' to something, you are always saying 'no' to something else. A 'yes' to attend a breakfast meeting might be a 'no' to your health, because it means you'll miss your morning run. A 'yes' to bringing forward a deadline so someone else can take an early holiday might be a 'no' to your family, because it means you need to stay later at work each night. A 'yes' to a networking event might be a 'no' to some much needed 'me time' to recharge your batteries.

While it's important to be giving and generous to others, it's important to keep the giving and receiving cycle in balance. Giving from a near empty cup will be fruitless. *Am I letting myself down by saying 'yes'?* is an important question.

A common reason people struggle with saying 'no' is because they can't find a good excuse at the time. The trap is thinking you must have an excuse! You are the only person who can set boundaries for your life, and they don't need to be explained every time you decide not to cross them. So next time someone asks you to do something, avoid searching for an excuse and just try one of these simple statements:

- ☐ *Thanks for the kind offer/invitation. I won't be able to take you up on it this time, but I wish you all the best.*
- ☐ *That sounds like a great opportunity, but I'll need to say 'no'.*
- ☐ *Thanks for thinking of me, but I won't be able to take that on.*
- ☐ *I can't do that right now, without something else falling off my schedule.*

With practice, it gets easier to say 'no'. It might help to start practising on email first, until you find the words that you can deliver confidently face to face. The important thing is to start somewhere, but focus on those requests that really can be done without you. Sure, it may be hard to try this for the first time on your boss when a list of demands hits your inbox, but there are undoubtedly many other things arising in your life where you do have the complete freedom of choice about your response.

Saying 'no' is really empowering! Once I knew how to say it in a way that felt half comfortable, it became a lot easier to do. I now think twice before saying 'yes' and I give careful consideration to what would be lost if I take something else on. It's opened so much space for me. I'm saying 'no' so much more now!

+ Can you say no?

Grab a piece of paper and list all of the things you are doing at the moment that you really don't want to be doing.

Why did you say 'yes'? Are some of these emotions behind your choice?

☐ Guilt

☐ Fear

☐ Responsibility

☐ Being agreeable

☐ Seeking approval

☐ Avoiding conflict

☐ Don't want to be judged

☐ Don't want to offend

☐ A sense of duty or obligation

☐ Other ...

+ Try this ... The 'no' note

Write yourself five 'no' notes for the week. These are permission slips to say 'no' to an offer, invitation, extra task or responsibility.

On a small piece of paper, write as follows:

I give myself permission to say 'no' to this: _____
(insert your signature)

Carry them in your pocket or wallet for the week. When you are faced with a situation that you know you should decline, mentally hand yourself one of your 'no' notes, then respond to the request with a polite and appropriately worded 'no'.

On the back of that 'no' note, write down all the things you gave back to yourself by saying 'no' to that request. Maybe it was time with your children, an opportunity to spend another two hours on something you really wanted to finish, or a peaceful night alone without taking any work home.

Eventually you will not need the notes. You will naturally assess the trade-offs and make a choice that is a 'yes' to the thing that matters most.

+ Try a Trade-off

If you are still stuck, try this. Before saying 'yes' to a new thing, identify something that you will give up. If you can't give up something, then don't take something on!

−+ −+

Creativity is the residue of time wasted.

−+ −+

Albert Einstein,
theoretical physicist

Exercise *17*
Busy Ban

-+ -+

What you focus on grows. You are as busy as you believe yourself to be.

Think about the last time you ran into a friend you hadn't seen for a while. We generally greet them and ask: *How are you?* Most people now answer with the response: *Soooooo busy!* Or invariably, the conversation will come round to all the things that make their life busy. It's such a common experience these days that people won't even wait for the answer, but will incorporate it into the question: *How are you . . . busy?* or *Are you having a busy day?* Try the response: *No, I'm not busy actually.* Then watch the look of surprise on their face!

This simple question that we greet each other with every day is meant to be an enquiry into another's happiness, health and wellbeing. In the past, people would have shared stories about what their children were doing, whether they had been on a trip, and any interesting changes at work.

Yes, we've always conversed about what we're doing but, somewhere in the last decade, the details have become unimportant. It's now just an interchange about the degree of busyness: *It's just crazy, I've got so much to do and I can never get through the list in a day!*

In this modern world, 'busy' is being worn as a badge of honour, a symbol of success, or a new way to display importance. Walk around a workplace and you'll see people rushing from one thing to another, talking about their back-to-back meeting schedule and how late they stayed up last night to clear the backlog. It creates a culture of expectation where even those who are on top of their work feel the pressure to appear busy, and eventually fall into the same traps of staying longer at work, checking emails all hours of the day and night, and rushing between tasks.

This attachment to being busy is a paradox. The stress and pressure is unpleasant, but we all seem to keep doing it. It's because ticking things off activates our brain's reward system. So does a sense of belonging and also receiving sympathy from a friend. So when you say *I'm so busy* and your friend responds *You poor thing*, it feels good. And this corrosive habit of busyness digs its claws into you a little bit more.

Researchers have discovered that people often feel busier than their diaries suggest they actually are.[1] It's the **thought** of all the things that have to be done that triggers the greatest sense of overload, stress and anxiety.

What you focus on grows. If you think and talk about how busy you feel, you'll feel busier and busier. When you focus on the endless list of tasks and the fast-moving treadmill, all you will notice is your lack of time and the rush of life.

+ What's your focus?

Do you do any of the following?

☐ Answer the question *How are you?* with a response that involves 'busy'

☐ Have conversations that eventually turn to the discussion of how busy you or the other person is

☐ Do things to look busy

☐ Think about how busy you are a number of times a day

☐ Feel weighed down when you think of how busy you are

☐ Feel important when you are busy

☐ Feel like you have to justify how you spent the day

☐ Wake up and go to sleep thinking about how busy you are

If you ticked three or more, your focus on busyness is high.

There is an alternative. When you change your thoughts, you change your actions, and this can change your life. A person who makes a choice not to focus on "busy", finds something else in its place: time, space, a sense of calm, a reconnection with the true pace of life, and the opportunity to once again choose what to do with the moments of downtime that are constantly on offer.

+ Try this . . . Busy ban

Remove the word 'busy' from your vocabulary. That means removing it from the words that come out of your mouth, and also the words floating through your mind.

Avoid conversations about how busy you or others are. When asked how you are, find another response such as:

☐ *I'm well, how are you?*

☐ *Focusing on the positives today!*

☐ *I'm feeling really inspired at the moment!*

☐ *I've been feeling quite energised. How are you feeling?*

☐ *Can't complain. It's a lovely day, isn't it?*

Not only will you have more interesting conversations, you'll experience the feelings you talk about!

But the biggest challenge is to erase the sense of busyness from your mind. It's just a matter of retraining your brain to find new pathways to get things done. Try these:

☐ When you find yourself thinking of all the things you need to do, just pick one thing and start doing it.

☐ When you start panicking about all the things you still have to do, remind yourself of what you have already achieved.

☐ When you have an idle moment but just can't get your mind off your to-do list, look at each task individually and ask yourself: *What can I learn today when I do that task?*

☐ When you wake in the morning, rather than thinking immediately of all the things you have to do, spend a few moments creating a sense of calm and space. Stretch your body, open the curtains and look at the sky then, as if you were waking a young child, ask yourself: *What exciting adventures will we have today!?*

Removing the word 'busy' will challenge you to come up with new ways to describe your life: exciting, full, an adventure, lots of opportunities to learn, lucky, inspiring, energising and enjoyable. And because what you focus on grows, you'll be surprised how different this can make you feel.

-+ -+

Happiness is a place between
too little and too much.

-+ -+

Finnish proverb

Exercise 18
Declutter

-+ -+

Less is more.

Are you craving a simpler life? If the life you've built creates stress and pressure, rather than space and freedom, it is possible to simplify it in small ways to reap big rewards.

When their house was being renovated many years ago, the family of four moved from a large five-bedroom house into a small two-bedroom workers' cottage. To be able to fit comfortably, they put everything into storage except the bare essentials. Four forks rather than the three sets of cutlery they owned for different occasions. Four plates that they washed between each meal. The kids shared a room, and the dining table was also the home-based office. The downsizing sounded quite daunting and they were unsure how the kids would react (they even had to select just two toys each to take to the cottage). But it had a surprising effect. They all loved the experience. Those four months gave them a taste of the simple life. A smaller house meant they didn't have so much to clean. A smaller wardrobe meant less time spent on: *What will I wear today?* And living in a small space fostered an even closer connection. To this day the kids still ask, 'When can we go back to the little house?'

Anyone who has done a spring-clean, tidied up their office, or culled unworn clothes from their wardrobe will know that, when you declutter, you feel lighter and clearer. Less things around you frees up your head space. Less things to do frees up your time. Less pressure and expectation frees up your spirit.

There is a growing trend of people changing their lives in ways that involve downsizing, so they can experience more connection and meaning. You don't have to go for a complete 'sea change' to declutter your life. Controlling your priorities, rather than letting the relentless onslaught of 'more' control you, is the first step towards getting your life in order.

Have you stopped to ask yourself: *How much do I actually need in my life? How much is enough?* Decluttering often starts with belongings, but opening your life up to more space also means decluttering your activities and your mind.

'I work full-time but I don't want to miss out on giving the kids all the support that non-working mothers give at school. So I am also on the tuckshop roster, help in the classroom and volunteer for the excursions. It means I'm up half the night, but at least I can say I give everything to my kids.' But she wasn't bringing her best to any of it. Always exhausted, she was rarely connected to anything she was doing, and she certainly wasn't happy.

There are three criteria that can help you answer the question *What's enough?*:

1. It brings joy.
2. It makes a difference.
3. It fulfils a need.

The first test for anything you are choosing to spend time on, think about, or accumulate should be whether it brings you a level of joy. Once something triggers resentment or other negative emotions, it's time to let it go. Even the 'ho-hum' of a neutral reaction tells you something. If an item of clothing doesn't make you feel great when you wear it, then why is it sitting in your wardrobe? If time spent with someone is frustrating and makes you feel put down, why are you with them? If circling thoughts are making you scared or sad, there are other things to focus on. Joy is a great indicator of what deserves to stay in your life and what should go.

Secondly, it should make a positive difference to your life or to someone else's. If a possession triggers great memories, then it plays a valuable role in your life. If something you're spending time thinking about produces a better way of serving your customers, then it is time well spent. But if you're attending an event out of obligation and know it will be two hours of wasted time, why are you letting it clutter up your evening?

Lastly of course, there will be things that fulfil a practical need. Possessions like a toothbrush, running shoes and a kettle. Activities like the grocery shopping, exercise, taking a shower or planning a future workshop. Many of our practical choices are made out of habit, so sometimes they need a fresh look to be sure they still fulfil a real need.

+ Try this . . . Declutter

Declutter all aspects of your life and watch the space for deeper reflection expand.

These criteria offer you an objective way to consider which of your belongings, your activities and your thoughts fit in your life, and when enough is enough:

☐ This brings me joy or uplifts me.

☐ This makes a difference to me or to someone I care about.

☐ This fulfils a practical need.

Let's see if they help you find more space in your life.

+ Declutter your stuff

Less things in your life means less money spent collecting them, less time spent maintaining them, and less expectation to get more. If you don't think you've got too much stuff, try this little experiment: open the second drawer in your kitchen. This is usually the place where all the extra utensils live and, over time, it can look like they've been breeding! If you find things you haven't used for ages, things you've forgotten you had, more than one of something, and mystery items that you no longer recognise, then you've got too much stuff. And this is only one drawer!

Walk through your home and other spaces like your office, and consider whether your belongings meet the criteria above. For the things that don't, consider who you could offer them to and how it could help them. It may be a family member, friends, colleagues or a charity. Feel the lightness that comes from having less, and the joy that comes from giving to others.

Before accumulating more, use the criteria to make sure that what you collect really belongs in your life.

+ Declutter your activity

Review all of your regular activities and commitments. Don't just focus on your work activities, but also consider your social life, family life, and all the little things that keep life moving. Use the criteria above to identify things that you don't need to be doing anymore.

Find your ideal weekly quota for things like:

- ☐ Social activities
- ☐ Exercise
- ☐ Number of things on your to-do list
- ☐ Extra-curricular activities for kids
- ☐ Housework
- ☐ Fillers like TV shows

Before you take on new activities, check them off against the criteria and only engage in the ones that are genuinely worthwhile.

+ Declutter your head

What's on your mind at the moment? Imagine each of these taking up precious real estate in your head. Using the criteria above, weed out the things that fall to the bottom of the list, write them down, and park the list in the bin! Now give your precious attention only to the things that you've decided add value.

Because thoughts are so recurrent, it's a good idea to declutter your head regularly by making this list every day. See how much you start to enjoy the feeling of tossing it in the bin!

-+ >

-+ -+

Most people do not listen with the intent to understand; they listen with the intent to reply.

-+ -+

Stephen Covey,
American author and business educator

Exercise 19
The Last Word

–+ –+

The world needs less problem-solvers, thinkers and doers,
and more listeners.

*T*here is amazing power in just listening. This silent and serene gift can heal, transform and inspire while you seemingly do, well, nothing! If you find it difficult to listen without other activities or thoughts interrupting, you are not alone.

Most people overestimate the quality of their listening. The simple fact is that the majority of people aren't great listeners. In one of the many studies confirming this, people were asked to sit through a ten-minute oral presentation, and then later recall its content. Half of the participants couldn't do it, even though it was only moments after the presentation. And 48 hours later, 75% failed to recall the content.[1] So as much as you might like to think you listen well, there is probably room for improvement. Let's see how you rate:

Which of the following have you caught yourself doing?

- [ ] Predicting what you think the other person will say
- [ ] Focusing on what you are going to say, rather than what's being said to you
- [ ] Misinterpreting something because you have filtered it through your own experiences or preferences
- [ ] Making assumptions about what others have said, because you weren't really listening
- [ ] Completely missing sections of what is being said
- [ ] Judging what's being said, rather than just hearing it
- [ ] Placing more importance on your views than those of others
- [ ] Assuming a role like problem-solver or advice-giver, without checking whether that was being sought from you
- [ ] Jumping into slight pauses in the conversation, in an attempt to divert it or wrap it up more quickly

There are a few different reasons why the simple human act of just listening can be so challenging to master.

Maybe you're too busy to put things down and just listen when someone else speaks. So you tuck the phone between your shoulder and your ear and keep typing, or putting away the dishes, or sorting your paperwork. Even when it's face to face, you rarely see two people conversing without another activity going on. In meeting rooms, some are writing notes or tapping on screens; at coffee shops, some hold their mobile devices and flick their eyes down. We know from multi-tasking studies that empathy levels drop dramatically when you multi-task, which is no surprise. You're missing all the subtle cues essential for true and deep communication.

But it's not just physical activity that invades during the act of listening. It's what's going on in your head. There may be something else on your mind, and if you're in a conversation that hasn't completely captured your attention, your brain naturally wanders back to more pressing concerns. Many a business person has been caught out this way in a meeting, thinking the topic isn't really relevant to them, then suddenly being asked a question. And how often has a family member been telling you about their day, but when they ask what you think, it's clear you've missed vital details. 'You're not listening!!' they rightly accuse you, and storm off.

Even if you are tuned in, the brain has another little trick that thwarts your intention to listen fully. The brain is a pattern-making machine, and it takes little pieces of information, fills in details from what it already has stored, and creates pictures in your head. So when your best friend returns from a trip to your favourite beach holiday spot and starts describing where they went for breakfast on the first morning, you're already three steps ahead, jumping in with, 'Oh, that's the one with the path right down to the sand. I love that place! Did you try the smoked salmon? They smoke it themselves and I spoke to the chef about how they do it!' You're not picturing **their** experience, you're picturing your own, and this becomes the source of all your comments.

While most friendly banter allows for these enthusiastic interruptions, your brain is just as likely to jump in like this when someone just desperately wants to be heard: 'I wish he would just listen! I barely get my last words out and he is jumping in trying to solve the problem. But it's not solutions I want. I just want to feel like he understands what I'm really saying.'

While wanting to help another person is a desire that comes from good intention, it ignores the value of simply listening and how healing that can be in its own right. Not only does it create space for the other person to fully express the message they are delivering to you, it creates the space for your brain to slow down, hear and comprehend more of what is being said, and connect that message to more insightful and emotionally-perceptive neural networks. It is likely that if you listen in this way to the very end of someone's words, your response will be just right.

+ Try this . . . The last word

Listening until the very last word has been uttered is harder than it might sound. It means listening with the intent to understand—not with the intent to comment, steer, advise or control. It means listening without interrupting, interjecting or talking over. But it also means listening without predicting or judging, without internal commentary and without drifting off. It means giving the gift of full attention.

It's important to recognise that the very nature of your attention means it will wander, and that is quite normal. But this exercise is excellent for training your brain to return quickly from its wanderings and back to the place that matters.

The trick with this exercise is to connect your attention fully with your sense of hearing. Whenever your mind drifts away, you'll notice that the sound of the person's voice becomes a bit less clear. When you direct your attention back to simply hearing the sound of their voice, it becomes crisper and more distinct again.

Most importantly, maintain the commitment to listening in this way right until the very last word of their last sentence. Don't even think about responding until that word has been heard. In the moment after, you will feel a natural space arise. Over time, you'll find the quality of your conversations deepen, you'll experience a smoother flow, and your contribution will be driven less by your fast-moving thoughts and more by your caring insights.

Aim to practise this at least five times each day. At first it may feel strange, but only because it's different. Eventually it will become natural, and you'll feel a lot more space grow around you.

−+ −+

The most beautiful experience we can
have is the mysterious . . . He to whom
this emotion is a stranger, who can
no longer pause to wonder and stand
rapt in awe, is as good as dead.

−+ −+

Albert Einstein,
theoretical physicist

Exercise 20
The Inner Pause Button

-+ -+

A simple breath, a pause, can make the world of difference.

*D*id you remember to breathe today? Sometimes it feels like there's not even time in the day to remember that! Lucky your subconscious brain looks after such basic functions. But don't underestimate the power of one simple breath to save the day, save your sanity, or even save a relationship.

If you're the sort of person who rushes through the day, dashing from one activity to the next without drawing breath, this exercise is for you. I bet your days pass by in a blur. You get heaps done, but then realise you forgot to make an important phone call, you haven't eaten, you got side-tracked when you were heading towards the toilet three hours ago and still haven't made it there, and now you're twelve minutes late for a client!

At times like this, wouldn't it be great if you had the ability to hit a pause button? A small pause in proceedings provides the space to clear a busy mind, to let your body catch up with your fast-moving thoughts, and to make a rational decision about what to do next. When you're busy, just ten seconds of space can feel like a holiday!

Well the good news is that you **do** have a pause button at your disposal. At any time, you can hit the inner pause button and interrupt the seemingly endless rush of thoughts and the oppressive sense of overwhelm. In that moment, you can rediscover your calm centre and reclaim your clarity and confidence.

She felt herself freeze. Overwhelmed with the busyness of the day, her head was full of all the things she needed to get done. She was beginning to panic. Her heart was racing and she couldn't think. And then she stopped and realised that she couldn't go on like this. She couldn't think straight. She was paralysed. So she decided to let it all go. A deep breathe in, and on the exhalation she let her shoulders fall loose, her forehead relax, and allowed the stress to drop away. The clutter seemed to clear, and now she was able to begin again. It was like starting afresh.

He felt things escalating. The blood was rushing to his temples, his hands were gripping the folder tightly, and he knew he was about to blow his top. But he stopped himself, not by holding it all in or trying to push it away, but by directing his attention to the flow of air through his nose and deep into his belly. Instead of following his frustration in circles around his head, he followed his breath on its

life-giving journey in and out of his body. And that one
small choice potentially changed the course of his life.

The stress response in your brain is rapid, often driving you to action before you've even had the chance to reflect on what you're doing. It is estimated that the rational part of the brain lags the emotional part by six seconds. This explains the all-too-common experience of firing off that curse email, only to wish seconds later there was a recall button. It's also why, on a day of many challenges, it's just the smallest thing that can trigger frustration or alarm. Stress and overwhelm can build throughout the day, and it doesn't take much for it to bubble over.

The most effective way to bring yourself out of the stress response is a deep and slow breath. This simple action activates your parasympathetic nervous system, which in turn slows your heartbeat and releases tension from your muscles. In fact, your breathing is the only element within this complex physiological system that you can control by choice, so it is the key to returning yourself to a state of calm.

The fact is that emotional reactions in your body must go through their cycle, and learning how to manage them is important. But it is just as important to realise how to let them go. It takes less than ninety seconds for an emotion to flood your bloodstream with chemicals, and for those chemicals to be flushed out.[1] But most emotions seem to last a lot longer, because we hold onto them—tossing around our thoughts and feelings, rather than letting them go.

By training yourself to press your inner pause button regularly, you strengthen your ability to regulate your emotional reactions, allowing time and space for a reset. Surprisingly, it only takes a matter of seconds to recover from the busyness that can overwhelm your mind, or the emotions that overtake your body. With practice, it takes just a moment to rediscover your clarity and focus.

+ Try this . . . The inner pause button

This is a simple exercise that involves introducing a very short 'mental intermission' between all sorts of activities that you undertake throughout your day. Don't wait until you're angry, frustrated, overwhelmed or out of control. Instead, get in the habit of injecting this pause between activities. When you make the pause a natural part of your day, you are more likely to use it when you are overtaken by emotion or overwhelmed by busyness.

Here are some great times to use your inner pause button:

- [ ] When you find yourself rushing
- [ ] When you are transitioning between activities that require different types of focus or response
- [ ] As you leave your house for the day, or as you leave your work space to attend a meeting
- [ ] When you are starting to juggle too many things at once and feel a growing sense of overwhelm
- [ ] When you notice rising frustration, anger, anxiety or fear
- [ ] When things are not turning out the way you expected

Here's a blow-by-blow explanation of how to do it. Remember, this is a mental pause. While it does not demand that you pause your physical movement at the same time, it can help to do so when you are first getting used to the practice.

Step 1   Recognise the need for a pause, and say to
yourself: *Time to push the pause button.*

Step 2   Bring your attention fully to your breath, tracking
the movement of two full breaths in and out. Break
it down by taking a deep breath in for two seconds,
holding it for one second, and letting it out for three
seconds. Take a moment to notice how your body
releases tension as the chemicals generated by your
emotions are allowed to flush out of your bloodstream.

Step 3   Switch your attention fully to what is in front
of you, leaving behind any thoughts, emotions or
distractions that have been taking hold of you.

Initially you will find that your attention wants to hold onto thoughts, emotions or distractions, so directing your attention to your breath may feel like a battle. But just work gently to notice your breath, even if it's just a split second of awareness. Over time, your ability to fully surrender to the gap that an inner pause offers will strengthen.

Aim to press your inner pause button at least five times every day. Eventually it will become natural and amazingly helpful.

-+ -+

The final mystery is oneself. When one
has weighed the sun in the balance,
and measured the steps of the moon
and mapped out the seven heavens
star by star, there still remains oneself.

-+ -+

Oscar Wilde,
Irish playwright, novelist and poet

Exercise 21
Making it Matter

-+ -+

Discipline brings freedom.

*T*he previous twenty exercises are designed to help you become familiar and comfortable with indulging in idle moments and intentionally doing less. These exercises can, and should, be repeated over and over. The true benefits unfold when you embrace them as habits in your daily life. You may initially find that many of them don't come naturally; but remember, you have probably spent many years training yourself into the habits you have now: busyness, doing too much, taking more on, keeping things moving, avoiding the void, or being attracted to action.

It is often said that it takes 21 days to build a habit, but the key is to simply repeat a new exercise regularly until it starts to feel comfortable, natural, and eventually becomes your default response in a situation. The biggest trap is to stop trying too early because you think it's not working. If you have the discipline to simply practise without pressure or expectation, one day you will be surprised by the changes you experience.

Routines matter, so incorporating simple disciplines into your day that create space, embrace stillness, celebrate silence and help you to slow down will set the foundation for a life of doing less and achieving more.

In this final exercise, it's time to bring it all together and design a life that allows you to truly do less and be more.

+ Step 1: Start as you intend to continue

Does your day start as you intend it to continue? Are the first 45 minutes of your day calm, centred, flowing with grace and ease, or do they resemble a hurricane crossing the coast?

It's an important reflection, because the first 45 minutes of your day set up the pathways that your brain and body will travel on for the rest of the day. Start with a crazy, busy routine and you will find yourself a long way down the road of stress, overwhelm and compulsive 'doing' before you've even left the house. But start the day with a sense of ease and flow, and your day is likely to continue in that manner.

I get out of bed much too late each day. I know it's because I stay up too late trying to catch up on all the chores and backlog from the day before. So by the time I finally drag myself out of bed, I'm running late. I never manage to fit breakfast in, because I start getting messages arriving on my mobile before I'm even fully dressed. Of course, I'm always running for the bus, and I'm so glad if I actually get a seat! That's when I get the chance to look at all the messages

properly and start replying, so that at least people aren't
waiting until I actually get into the office. When my bus
arrives at my stop, I already feel exhausted. Sometimes on
the walk from there to the office, I think maybe I should
look for another job.

There is another way. Those who find some time to appreciate their morning often report feeling happier throughout the day. So how can you create a sense of ease and flow by rethinking the first parts of your day?

+ Try this . . . Mornings matter

Take the 'doing' out of the first 45 minutes of your day and create a routine that incorporates all of the following:

1. Move your body—this could be stretching, yoga, dancing, walking, running or playing with the kids.
2. Clear your mind—this could be spending some time in nature, a morning meditation, a quiet and mindful breakfast routine, or simply a few deep breaths. As part of this practice, set an intention for the day. You can do this by simply asking a question like: *How can I be of service today?*
3. Connect—with your loved ones and with yourself. Instead of rushing past your family members, take the time to connect. A seven-second hug can release enough oxytocin to put you on a high for the rest of the day. And connect with yourself by doing something pleasant that makes you smile and laugh. This also releases feel-good chemicals, setting you up for a positive day.

By all means resist the lure of technology. While you may argue that it is a form of connection or a source of fun, it makes your brain move fast and shallowly, and takes you away from a connection with yourself.

I shook up my whole morning. Oversleeping was generating a level of busyness that I just couldn't sustain throughout the day. So I now get out of bed earlier and resist the temptation to look at my mobile before 9am. I even use the bus trip to deepen my relaxation, and often gaze out the window and watch the world pass by. I couldn't find the time to do an hour of exercise, so I go out to the hill close to home and do ten minutes of really fast walking. It gets my heart pumping and I feel amazing after it. Some mornings I manage five minutes of meditation and it makes the world of difference. I feel great and my day unfolds better. The interesting side effect is that the messages on my mobile have slowed down too.

+ Step 2: Create space for your mind

The world is awakening to an understanding that ancient traditions have had since the beginning of time. There are many benefits to be had from sitting with stillness and in silence. Various studies on meditation reveal that even twenty minutes a day over an eight-week period can have some incredible results. From preserving performance in the ageing brain, to enhancing compassion, decreasing depression and boosting learning, meditation seems to be a balm for every modern-day ailment.[1]

Given the evidence that now exists on the benefits of contemplative practice, you would imagine that every person in the world would be signing up to be part of it. While the uptake is definitely on the rise, many people still struggle with the idea of sitting in silence and stillness.

'I can't meditate!' she said definitively, like there was a pass or fail element to the practice. 'I have too many thoughts. No matter how hard I try, I can't get rid of them!' And like many others she was missing the point. You see, it is impossible to have no thoughts. In fact, the human brain throws up a thought roughly every six to ten seconds. A goal of meditation is not to eliminate all thoughts, but to learn how to observe them, let them pass, and strengthen your ability to redirect your attention back to the present. If you need to do that a hundred times in five minutes, then that really is okay!

+ Try this . . . Meditation matters

It might take a while for your mind to slow down, so consider breaking your practice into these three stages:

Stage 1:   Find a place in your house where you can sit comfortably for a period of time. Schedule a time where you can sit uninterrupted for fifteen minutes. During this time, simply pay attention to what your mind is doing. Watch your mind as if you were watching TV. What channel is on? What screen is playing? What stories are running through it? Do this with no judgement, expectation or aspiration—your only goal is to watch your thoughts. Try this every day for a week.

Stage 2: Again, try this every day for a week. Build in a fifteen-minute period of silent retreat. Allocate this time in the period after you've done your day's work and before you ease into the evening routine. Disconnect from all distractions, noises and interruptions. You can use this time to practise meditating, or undertake a simple physical activity like walking, ironing, or sipping a cup of tea. Just be sure the activity you choose is soothing, not overly stimulating.

Stage 3: Build up a meditation practice. On the first day, simply spend one minute meditating on your breath. Sit in a quiet place and focus your attention on lengthening your inhalation and your exhalation. Breathe in slowly for four counts, hold for four, breathe out for four and hold for four. If your mind wanders (which it will quite regularly!), just circle it gently back from wherever it has wandered to once again pay attention to your breath. You will notice the chatter in your mind subside for that short time when you are attending to your breath.

Every day add one more minute to your meditation, until you are meditating for fifteen minutes a day.

+ Step 3: Keep doing the things that matter

Throughout this book we've encouraged you to try as many exercises as possible to create the space for insights, ideas and inspiration to hit. Even if you feel you have perfected an exercise, unless you continue to intentionally maintain it as a regular practice in your life, its effects will fade.

But even habits can become mindless, so the real key is to regularly challenge yourself with something new and different.

+ Try this . . . Repetition matters

Choose three exercises that you add to your daily life for at least the next three months. You might choose the ones you found had the most impact when you tried them, or you might choose the ones you feel deserve a bit more time and effort. It's totally up to you to decide what fits best with your life now, but also which exercises will take you closer to living the life you really want.

Once you've made your choices, repeat these exercises as often as possible, and stick with them for the full three months, regardless of whether you think they make any difference. Rewiring your brain is like planting a new garden. Just placing the seeds in the ground does not make them suddenly bloom. That takes constant nourishment and attention, then suddenly one day you wake to a bed of roses! So trust that your regular application of an exercise will reap rewards somewhere, and just do it.

After three months, swap your three exercises for new ones. This doesn't mean you'll stop the previous ones, because they may now be really helpful habits embedded in your life. But do make an intentional switch to adopt three new exercises that you will practice repeatedly to discover what other benefits are still possible.

Final words . . .

-+ -+

W e hope you have cracked open the door and reconnected with your own steady source of wisdom, patience and insight. Remember to always take time out, dream big, and do it now!

> *We shall not cease from exploration*
> *And the end of all our exploring*
> *Will be to arrive where we started*
> *And know the place for the first time.*

from *Four Quartets* by T.S. Eliot, British poet

References

-+ -+

+ Chapter 2

1   Wilson TD, Reinhard DA, Westgate EC, Gilbert DT, Ellerbeck N, Hahn C, Brown CL & Shaked A (2014) 'Just think: the challenges of the disengaged mind', *Science*, July, Vol 345, No 6192, pp 75-77
2   Robinson, Evan (2015) 'Why crunch modes doesn't work: six lessons' for *International Game Developers Association*
3   Janssen CP, Gould SJJ, Li SYW, Brumby DR & Cox AL (2015) 'Integrating knowledge of multi-tasking and interruptions across different perspectives and research methods', *International Journal of Human-Computer Studies*, 79, pp 1-5
4   Kyung Hee Kim (2011) 'The creativity crisis: the decrease in creative thinking scores on the Torrance Tests of Creative Thinking', *Creativity Research Journal*, 23:4, pp 285-295
5   Kaufman, Scott (2014) 'Dreams of glory', *Psychology Today*, March 11

+ Exercise 1

1   Manhart, C (2004) 'The limits of multi-tasking', *The Scientific American Mind*
2   Ophira E, Nass C & Wagner, AD (2009) 'Cognitive control in media multitaskers', *Proceedings of the National Academy of Sciences*, Vol 106, No 33, August 25
3   Meyer D E & Kieras D E (1997) 'A computational theory of executive cognitive processes and multiple-task performance: Part 1. Basic mechanisms', *Psychological Review, 104*, 3-65.
4   Janssen CP, Gould SJJ, Li SYW, Brumby DR & Cox AL (2015) 'Integrating knowledge of multi-tasking and interruptions across

different perspectives and research methods', *International Journal of Human-Computer Studies*, 79, pp 1-5

5   Loh KK & Kanai, R (2014) 'High media multi-tasking is associated with smaller grey-matter density in the anterior cingulate cortex', *Plos One*, 24 September

+ Exercise 3

1   Kirste I, Nicola Z, Kronenberg G, Walker T, Liu R & Kempermann G (2013) 'Is silence golden? Effects of auditory stimuli and their absence on adult hippocampal neurogenesis', *Brain Structure and Function*, December

+ Exercise 7

1   See more at https://cs.stanford.edu/people/eroberts/cs181/projects/crunchmode/econ-crunch-mode

2   Person, Taylor (2016) 'The only 3 ways to be more productive', *Entrepreneur*, July 19

3   Kivimäki, Mika et al. (2015)'Long working hours and risk of coronary heart disease and stroke: a systematic review and meta-analysis of published and unpublished data for 603,838 individuals', *The Lancet*, Volume 386, Issue 10005, pp 1739-1746

4   The Sydney Morning Herald (2015) 'The 38-hour week a rarity among full-time workers, new data shows' October 28

5   Eisenberg, Richard (2016) 'Sweden's intriguing 6-hour workday experiment' *Forbes*, June 7

+ Exercise 8

1   Dijksterhuis A, Bos MW, Nordgren LF & van Baaren RB (2006) 'On making the right choice: the deliberation-without-attention effect', *Science* Feb 17, 311(5763), pp 1005-7

+ Exercise 9

1   Find out more about Francesco Cirillo's Pomodoro Method at http://cirillocompany.de

+ Exercise 10

1   Mann S & Cadman R (2014) 'Does being bored make us more creative?' *Creativity Research Journal*, Volume 26, Issue 2

+ Exercise 11

1   Berman MG, Kross E, Krpan KM, Askren MK, Burson A, Deldin PJ, Kaplan S, Sherdell L, Gotlib IH & Jonides J (2012) 'Interacting with nature improves cognition and affect for individuals with depression', *Journal of Affective Disorders*, November, 140(3), pp 300-305

2   Ulrich RS (1984) 'View through a window may influence recovery from surgery', *Science*, 27 April, Vol 224, Issue 4647, pp 420-421

3   Cho, Renee (2011) 'Why we must reconnect with nature', *State of the Planet*, Columbia University, May 26

+ Exercise 12

1   Find out more about the science of play at the National Institute for Play http://www.nifplay.org

2   View award-winning innovator Tom Wujec's TED talk on the benefits of the marshmallow challenge at www.ted.com/talks/tom_wujec_build_a_tower.html

+ Exercise 17

1   Giang, Vivian (2014) 'How everything we tell ourselves about how busy we are is a lie', *Fast Company*, September 5

+ Exercise 19

1   Sullivan B & Thompson H (2013) 'Now hear this! most people stink at listening', *Scientific American Mind*, 3 May

+ Exercise 20

1   Bolte Taylor, J (2009) *My Stroke of Insight: A Brain Scientist's Personal Journey*, Hodder Paperback

+ Exercise 21

1   Hofmann SG, Grossman P & Hinton DE (2011) 'Loving-kindness and compassion meditation: potential for psychological interventions', *Clinical Psychology Review*, 31(7), pp 1126-1132 doi:10.1016/j.cpr.2011.07.003

ABOUT THE AUTHORS

© Tanya Love Portrait

Susan Pearse will change the way you think. A quarter life crisis, a shopping trip to New York, and a chance meeting with His Holiness the Dalai Lama lead to the discovery of her life's purpose: to wake up the world. She swapped clothes shopping for spiritual shopping, exploring everything from quantum physics and neuroscience, to crystals and chakras. She found one core truth that she now teaches people in all walks of life: the need to get out of your head and fully connect with your life. Her passion is to teach people the power and skill of being in the present moment, in business and in life.

Susan is regularly called on by the media to share her tips for mindful living. She is a sought-after speaker, and writes for the Huffington Post. She is on the Development Board of the Queensland Brain Institute, a world leading organisation in brain research based in Australia.

As a working mother and entrepreneur, Susan understands the challenges of juggling a busy and rewarding career while maintaining a fulfilling family life. Susan lives in Brisbane with her family.

Martina Sheehan is best known for opening people's eyes to the power of their mind. Whether it was just in her nature, or because of a near-death experience in her childhood, she has always sought to understand the deeper nature of things. Graduating from university with a degree in engineering was just the first step in her journey to discover what really makes us tick. She's very glad she never achieved her childhood dream of becoming an astronaut, realising it's the magic and mayhem on earth that still cries out for exploration and understanding. Instead, she's a pioneer at the final frontier: the human mind. Her great passion is to teach people the truth about the precious gift of attention. Martina has run her own successful businesses for over fifteen years, and is a trusted guide for those who know it's time to live and work with deeper connection and greater purpose. She is renowned for finding the right tone to open the minds of leaders to deep truths often overlooked in the business world, and she is regularly invited to speak at conferences.

www.mindgardener.com

Hay House Titles of Related Interest

YOU CAN HEAL YOUR LIFE, the movie,
starring Louise Hay & Friends
(available as a 1-DVD program and an expanded 2-DVD set)
Watch the trailer at: www.LouiseHayMovie.com

THE SHIFT, the movie,
starring Dr. Wayne W. Dyer
(available as a 1-DVD program and an expanded 2-DVD set)
Watch the trailer at: www.DyerMovie.com

-+ -+ -+ -+ -+

BREAKING THE HABIT OF BEING YOURSELF:
How to Lose Your Mind and Create a New One,
by Dr. Joe Dispenza

E-SQUARED:
Nine Do-It-Yourself Energy Experiments That Prove Your
Thoughts Create Your Reality, by Pam Grout

THE POWER OF INTENTION:
Learning to Co-create Your World, Your Way,
by Dr. Wayne W. Dyer

THE MOTIVATION MANIFESTO:
9 Declarations to Claim Your Personal Power,
by Brendon Burchard

GETTING REAL ABOUT HAVING IT ALL:
Be Your Best, Love Your Career and Bring Back Your Sparkle,
by Megan Dalla-Camina

All of the above are available at www.hayhouse.co.uk

-+ -+ -+ -+ -+

Notes

Notes

_____

_____

_____

_____

_____

_____

_____

_____

_____

_____

_____

_____

Notes

Notes

_____

_____

_____

_____

_____

_____

_____

_____

_____

_____

_____

_____

_____

HAY HOUSE

Look within

Join the conversation about latest products, events, exclusive offers and more.

 Hay House UK

 @HayHouseUK

 @hayhouseuk

 healyourlife.com

We'd love to hear from you!